SOURCES IN THE HISTORY OF INTERPRETATION, 2

Lectures on the

Reunion of the Churches

DÖLLINGER

LECTURES ON THE REUNION OF THE CHURCHES

Johann Josef Ignaz von Döllinger

ALEPH  PRESS

ALEC R. ALLENSON, INC.
Naperville, Illinois

1973

ISBN 0-8401-0567-3

Library of Congress Catalog Card No. 74-131579

Printed in the United States of America

JOHANN JOSEF IGNAZ VON DÖLLINGER, 1799-1890, of Munich, the leading Catholic church historian in nineteenth-century Germany, became, the year after his ordination in 1822, professor of ecclesiastical history and canon law at Aschaffenburg. From 1826 until the fall of Abel's ultramontane party in 1847 he was professor of theology at the University of Munich; in 1849 he was reinstated as professor of ecclesiastical history. He was elected Rector Magnificus in 1867 and made president of the Bavarian Academy of Sciences in 1873. While his most extensive works are not translated, fourteen titles have appeared in English. From 1861 onwards he publicly asserted that the temporal sovereignty of the pope was not the true basis of the church, and for a decade he was the leading opponent of the ultramontane position. After the promulgation of papal infallibility in 1870, Döllinger sent his refusal to subscribe to Abp. von Scherr on March 29th, 1871, and the *excommunicatio maior* was pronounced against him on April 17th. Although he never formally joined the German Old Catholic Church, he chaired the Bonn Reunion Conferences of 1874 and 1875. In 1874, writing to Pastor Widmann, he declared 'that I belong by conviction to the Old Catholic Community' in its threefold vocation of maintaining the truth as held by the early church, of becoming a church free from delusion and superstition, and of serving 'as an instrument and a link of mediation for a future greater reunion of the disunited Christians and Churches.' *(Declarations and letters on the Vatican decrees,* 1891, p. 117-18). Against the charge that he was sulking in seclusion, he had replied in 1868 that 'I follow the course of affairs calmly and attentively, and I strive daily to supplement and correct my knowledge... But do you call this "sulking"? If so, then St. Bernard, Fénelon — and how many others! — were also in sulky corners in their time.' *(Declarations,* p. 174). At his death he again refused to submit and was attended by Prof. Friedrich. The seven lectures *Über die Wiedervereinigung der christlichen Kirchen,* delivered early in 1872, were inaccurately reported in the *Allgemeine Zeitung;* Döllinger, unable to prepare them for publication, made the MS available to Henry Nutcombe Oxenham (1829-1888, received by Manning into the Roman Catholic Church in 1857) for translation into English. A New York issue of the London edition was published by Pott, Young & Co. in 1872; the German text appeared in 1888.

Lectures

ON THE

Reunion of the Churches

By JOHN J. I. VON DÖLLINGER, D.D., D.C L.,

PROFESSOR OF ECCLESIASTICAL HISTORY IN THE UNIVERSITY OF MUNICH,
PROVOST OF THE CHAPEL-ROYAL, ETC. ETC.

TRANSLATED WITH PREFACE

By HENRY NUTCOMBE OXENHAM, M.A.,

LATE SCHOLAR OF BALLIOL COLLEGE, OXFORD

'*Et ingressus est in ea spiritus, et vixerunt; steteruntque super pedes suos exercitus grandis nimis valde. Et dixit ad me; Fili hominis, ossa hæc universa domus Israel est.*'

RIVINGTONS
London, Oxford, and Cambridge
1872

To the

Rev. HENRY PARRY LIDDON, D.D., D.C.L.,

IRELAND PROFESSOR OF EXEGESIS IN THE UNIVERSITY OF OXFORD,
CANON OF ST. PAUL'S.

MY DEAR LIDDON,

You will readily believe that there are many reasons why I should gladly seize the opportunity of dedicating this volume to you, but it will be sufficient to mention two. In the first place, it has long been my wish to put on record some acknowledgment of a friendship which has now lasted nearly twenty-five years, dating from my first undergraduate term at Oxford, and which has been to me the source of so much happiness and so many blessings. Yet what could I hope to offer of my own that would be at all worthy of your acceptance? Here, however, where for the most part the language alone is mine, and the thoughts are those of one whom we have both learned to love and reverence, is something which I may not unfitly present and you need not hesitate to accept. And then, again, I would ask you to welcome this Dedication, as a little souvenir of the pleasant and profitable hours we spent together last year at Munich in the company of the illustrious author.

Wishing you every blessing, and praying that you may long be spared with health and strength to labour in your place for those sacred interests, so dear to both of us, to which Dr. Döllinger has here devoted the ripe wisdom of his maturest reflections,

    I am ever, my dear Liddon,

        Most affectionately yours,

            H. N. OXENHAM.

NATIVITY OF OUR LADY, 1872.

CONTENTS.

	PAGE
PREFACE,	ix

LECTURE I.

GENERAL REVIEW OF THE RELIGIOUS CONDITION OF THE WORLD, ... 1

LECTURE II.

THE DUTY OF CHRISTIAN NATIONS TO THE HEATHEN, AND ITS GREAT HINDRANCE, ... 20

LECTURE III.

DIVISION OF EAST AND WEST: GROUNDS OF HOPE, . 32

LECTURE IV.

THE GERMAN REFORMATION, ... 60

LECTURE V.

REACTION TOWARDS UNION ON THE CONTINENT IN THE SEVENTEENTH CENTURY, ... 84

LECTURE VI.

THE ENGLISH REFORMATION, ITS NATURE AND RESULTS, . 103

LECTURE VII.

DIFFICULTIES AND GROUNDS OF HOPE, . . . 136

PREFACE.

SOME apology is due to the public both for the delay in the appearance of this work, and for the form in which it is now presented to them. The Lectures here translated were delivered by Dr. Döllinger in the Great Hall of the Museum at Munich, on Friday evenings, during the months of February and March last; but it was his intention to revise and enlarge them considerably before publication, and he had kindly promised to send me the sheets for translation, as they were successively printed off. But meanwhile the execution of this design has been delayed beyond his expectation by the pressure of other engagements, and he therefore afterwards offered to supply me with the manuscript of the Lectures, as originally delivered, from which the present translation has been made. I shall, of course, hereafter avail myself of the complete work on its appearance in Germany, should occasion arise for doing so. It is right to add that none of the reports of the course which appeared in the principal German newspapers, and were wholly or partially reproduced in some of our own, were published with the author's sanction, and that he disclaims all responsibility for them. The actual text differs in many respects from the report in the *Allgemeine Zeitung*. This is accordingly the first appearance of the Lectures, either in Germany or in England, in an authentic form. Some notes and references the author has himself added to the manuscript. For all *bracketed* notes I am alone responsible. They are for the most part simply designed to provide illustrative details of information, which may not always be familiar to the general reader.

The momentous question which Dr. Döllinger has here undertaken to discuss, and to which indeed he has again and again called attention in several of his previous works, is one that has long been forcing itself on the thoughts of serious men in all parts of our divided Christendom. Some testimonies to the widespread and growing sense of its importance have been collected, as well from Catholic as from Anglican writers, in a former work of mine on the subject, and the evidence might be indefinitely multiplied.¹ Within the last few years only, to such names as Wiseman, Ketteler, and Dupanloup have been added those of men differing as widely in many respects both from them and from each other, as Maret, Gratry, Perreyve, Michaud, Strossmayer, and the martyred Darboy. Nor is the feeling, as will be seen from these Lectures, confined to one side only. It is shared also by Lutheran as well as Anglican divines, though probably not as yet to the same extent by the former.²

We cannot wonder that it should be so. The direct contradiction to the will and purpose of our divine Lord, revealed in the religious divisions of His professed disciples, would of course alone be a more than sufficient motive for making every exertion to put an end to a state of things so displeasing to Him. But over and above this, the overwhelming practical interest of the question is impressing, I might say obtruding, itself

¹ See Appendix to my *Letter to F. Lockhart on Dr. Pusey's Eirenicon*, 2d ed., Washbourne, 1872.
² See, *e.g.*, some remarkable letters addressed by several Protestant pastors to Bishop Martin of Paderborn, urging him to use his influence for the removal of what they allege to be the two chief hindrances to a reunion of the separated Churches, viz., the compulsory celibacy of the clergy and the withdrawal of the chalice from the people. The letters are given in the second appendix to Friedrich's *Tagebuch während des Vat. Concils*, pp. 424 *sqq.*

more prominently every day on the notice even of the most superficial observers of the existing phenomena, whether of the Christian or the Heathen world. On the latter point nothing need be added here to what has been so fully set forth by the lecturer. The single fact that, at the end of eighteen centuries, some 800,000,000 of our fellow-men—considerably over two-thirds of the human race—are still strangers to any form of Christianity, speaks volumes. And it is not the less, but the more significant, when we call to mind the large and generous efforts which have been made for their conversion during the last three centuries,—the immense expenditure of English gold with such absurdly disproportionate results, and the heroic labours of Catholic missionaries, who have shed their blood like water on almost every shore, and yet have gathered in but a precarious harvest of souls, counted by hundreds or thousands, when the millions of heathendom should long since have become obedient to the faith. It was not thus when Apostles preached, when Augustine, or Boniface, or Columba went forth to win whole nations to the Gospel. And why not? They taught a "common Christianity" in a very different sense from that now attached to the phrase, and the world, beholding their unity, believed in Him who sent them. But the rival preachers of a score of jarring creeds the world cannot believe in; and for the most part it cuts the knot by rejecting all alike. We were warned beforehand that it must be so.

I will but add the eloquent testimony of Bishop Maret on this point: "If, after eighteen centuries, idolatry prevails over the greater part of the globe; if Mahometism desolates once flourishing Christian countries; if a thinly disguised atheism ravages even the Christian world,—doubt not that one of the most powerful causes of so many moral and social miseries, so many shameful humiliations, lies in the many unhappy internal divisions of Christians, which constitute schism and heresy. If the Eastern Churches were reunited to the Mother Church, if our brethren, separated from unity by the violent revolutions of the sixteenth century, were reunited with us, what a new power of transformation and victory would Christianity display in the world, combining in one all its living forces, all the elements of regenerated progress, science, and civilisation. Then indeed should we witness the reign of God and of His Christ on earth. Everything which can hinder the drawing together again of hearts and minds, and the restoration of religious unity, should be regarded as the greatest of evils, because it is what hinders the greatest of blessings."[1]

And if we turn our glance on the Christian world, the portentous results of disunion stare us yet more visibly in the face. Scepticism manifests its presence daily and hourly among us in a thousand open or insidious forms. It colours our literature, it controls our policy, it mounts our pulpits, it aspires to restrain or to formulate our prayers. And how do the champions of orthodoxy essay to meet it? By ingenious arguments, which perhaps only half convince themselves; by stammering appeals to an undefined authority; or by the worn-out sophisms of "the Bible and the Bible only" theory, as though the world could stand on the tortoise, and the tortoise stand upon space. But this will not avail. Protestantism, as a system of positive belief, is found to be unequal to the crisis.[2] If I refer to the independent witness of a recent writer in the *West-*

[1] *Du Concile Général*, vol. ii. pp. 387, 8.

[2] It is a fact abundantly proved by statistics that religious perplexity is one main cause of the large increase of insanity in modern times, as also that suicide is more common in Protestant than in Catholic countries.— See Casper's *Denkwürdigkeiten zur medicin. Statistik*, quoted in Buckle's *History of Civilisation*, vol. i. p. 26.

minster Review, it is not for any novelty in his argument —for it has often been urged before—still less from any sympathy with his tone, even where I am able to agree with him; but simply because he has defined the situation from the infidel point of view with edifying candour and precision.[1]

Catholicism, he begins by assuring us, is destined to outlive Protestantism, as well because " its promises are more satisfactory to the instincts of the vulgar"—that is, because it better satisfies the religious cravings of the human soul—as from its resting on a more philosophical basis. He is reviewing Dr. Newman's recent reprint of the 85th of the *Tracts for the Times*, vindicating the claims of historical as opposed to what is sometimes called Bible Christianity, and he fully admits the force of the argument. He thinks it certain that " at the date of the publication of the fourth Gospel, or very shortly afterwards," which can hardly mean later than the second century, the teaching of the Church was distinctively Catholic, and reminds us that the earliest authorities cited for the canon of Scripture are equally emphatic in asserting, *e.g.*, the doctrines of the Eucharistic sacrifice and prayer for the dead. He

[1] *West. Rev.* for July 1872 : Art. " Difficulties of Protestantism."

is naturally not sanguine as to the future spread of Christianity, and refers for his own purposes to the comparative failure, which was noticed just now, of modern missionary efforts. But he is quite convinced that, wherever it does spread, it will not be in the form of Protestantism. Indeed, he goes so far as to express an opinion that, "speaking broadly, it is impossible now-a-days to *convert* any one to" a system, which cannot elicit faith, for it is in fact simply "an arrested development of free thought," and is already writhing uneasily under the artificial fetters imposed on it at the Reformation. It is incapable from its nature of forming a permanent dwelling-place for the mind, but has done good service as a temporary resting-place, "which has happily sheltered man on his way from bondage to freedom, from darkness to light, from theology to Truth." In other words, it has served to break, and thereby to disguise, the fall from Christian faith into naked infidelity. The reviewer urges in conclusion, what is obvious, that the final issue must turn on the admission or denial of the supernatural in any form; and he might have added that premonitory signs are already discernible of the approach of the contest, if it is not actually begun. That the contending forces will be

Preface. xvii

eventually driven by the conditions of the conflict to range themselves in two, and two only, camps, under the rival banners of faith or of unbelief, there cannot be a doubt, and as little that such a crisis would involve "not only the eclipse, but the disappearance of the system known as Protestantism," through the absorption of its positive and negative elements into the opposite systems to which they respectively belong.

There are two reasons just now for insisting on this aspect of the case, and which have led me to dwell, at greater length than its intrinsic merits would require, on the article in the *Westminster Review*. In the first place, it is well that religious Protestants should bring themselves to understand distinctly—and I use the term, "Protestant," for all who rest their belief on the Protestant principle of private judgment, as distinct from the traditional and historical basis of Catholic Christianity—on how insecure a tenure they hold those portions of revealed truth which they are sincerely anxious to retain, and how signal must be their discomfiture, if they elect to stand alone against the advancing forces of unbelief.[1] It should be borne in

[1] A studiously vague and general assertion of the supernatural element in religion was only carried by a majority of 61 to 46 last June in the Synod of the French Protestant Church, after a prolonged and stormy

mind that Protestantism, when left to itself, has always betrayed an inherent tendency to gravitate towards Socinianism. This has been abundantly illustrated in the Reformed Churches of Germany and Switzerland, while a case tried before the English law courts some forty years ago brought out the startling fact, that almost the entire Presbyterian body in this country had abandoned the fundamental tenet which discriminates Christianity from natural religion.[1]

And it is surely not a little significant in this connexion that, in the vital controversy now agitating the Established Church, the Evangelical party, whose theological culture has never been their strong point, should have openly and somewhat eagerly joined the ugly rush against that majestic and venerable formulary which most effectively guards the central verity of revelation. The circumstance is the more remarkable, because the Athanasian Creed touches on no single doctrine which they do not, equally with their High Church and Ritualist rivals, profess to believe. And it would be the merest excess, not of charity, but of unreason, to affect to doubt that, with the great majo-

debate of several days' duration. It contains no distinct assertion of the divinity of Christ.

[1] The case of Lady Hewley's Charity, in 1832.

Preface. xix

rity of the assailing party, the real ground of antagonism lies in a disbelief, more or less consciously acknowledged, either of some of the doctrinal statements of the Creed, or of its peremptory assertion of a principle, borne out by every line of the New Testament, that men will be held responsible for their acceptance of God's revelation no less than for their obedience to His moral law.[1]

Scarcely less suggestive than the Evangelical attitude towards the Athanasian Creed, is the line taken by (I fear) the great body of English Dissenters on the Education question, which inevitably reminds one of the advice of the false mother in Solomon's judgment. Better that all our children should be brought up in an "unsectarian" religion—that is, without any faith at all—than that any of them should be taught the Apostles' Creed, which happens to be a distinctive formulary of two, not inconsiderable, Christian "denominations."[2] Such a system is a far more serious

[1] It is worth remarking that those Protestant communities which have dropped the Athanasian Creed have, as a rule, either retained a very faltering hold on the doctrine of the Holy Trinity, or abandoned it altogether. The American Episcopal Church cannot fairly be quoted as an exception, for—not to insist on the necessarily conservative influence of a hierarchy—it is not yet a century old, and there is understood to be a growing desire among its more orthodox members for the restoration of what was hastily cast away in an age which, to say the least, gave a peculiar prominence to the negative side of its beliefs.

[2] Since the above passage was written, it has received a striking con-

xx *Preface.*

evil, both in theory and practice, than pure secularism, for it not only omits all genuine religious teaching, but supplants it by a spurious substitute. And there is a further reason for noticing the matter here, because " the religious difficulty " of education, of which we have heard so much during the last few years, is notoriously and solely due to the divided state of Christendom. But for that, we should never have heard of the strange undertaking to construct, what one of the Anglican Bishops the other day justly termed " a new religion," viz., the theological residuum extracted by eliminating whatever is distinctive in the teaching of any of the hundred or so of, I was

firmation in the report of a debate on the subject in the Wesleyan Conference, extending over two days and ending in a drawn battle (see *Times* of August 14 and 15). The Wesleyans have usually been regarded as denominationalists, but with many of them the desire for a *privilegium* against Anglican and Roman Catholic schools appears to have overpowered every other feeling. Those who supported the resolution against denominational education dwelt avowedly, and almost exclusively, on the argument that it enabled " Papists " and Anglicans to train their children in their own faith. As the mover of the resolution (Rev. W. Arthur) put it, " Their choice lay between Popery and the Bible." It is right to say that several ministers spoke on the other side, one of whom (Rev. E. E. Jenkins), honestly avowed that "he would rather have the Bible explained to a child of his in a Ritualist or Broad Church school than have it simply read in a cold and lifeless manner in a school where no explanation was given. He would rather be a Papist than an Atheist or a Unitarian." This is the language both of Christianity and of common sense; if the Bible is to be read in school without note or comment, it had much better be read in Hebrew.

Preface.

going to say, Christian sects in the country.[1] But, in presence of Jews and Secularists, it may well be questioned if the existence of a personal God must not be relegated to the forbidden category of "denominational" beliefs; about the divinity of Christ there is confessedly no question at all. And the education difficulty has its political as well as its religious side. If a Roman Emperor wished that his people had but one neck, a modern statesman might with better reason wish, on the lowest ground, that they had but one religion.

It has, indeed, been suggested that what is really wanted, and is alone practicable, is "a better management of our differences." And it is well, no doubt, to cultivate friendly relations with those from whom we differ, so far as it can be done without any compromise of principle. A better understanding between the members of divided communions is the first step, as

[1] Bishop Magee, whose speech is referred to in the text, speaks of "126 religious fractions of the country."—See *Guardian* for July 24, 1872. It is gratifying to learn that this hopeful experiment is actually about to be tried in Japan, where it is announced that "the Government has decided on the promulgation of *a new form of religion*, after careful consultation with the most noted exponents of each sect, *and all will be compelled to conform thereto.* The new religion will be *enlightened, simple,* and *adapted to common sense,* and is likely to meet the approval of all classes." Perhaps it may; the Japanese are said to be about the most irreligious and immoral people on the face of the earth.

the lecturer has pointed out, towards the desired reconciliation; the first, but not the last. To coalesce on a basis of mutual disagreement,

> "Thou, for my sake, at Alla's shrine,
> And I at any god's, for thine,"

is one thing; it is quite another to meet in the unity of a common faith. The rule of "liberty in what is doubtful, and charity in all things" is most excellent, as far as it goes, but it will secure no inward or lasting harmony between those who are at variance on the essential truths of revelation. Had the early Church been united, in its stand against the Pagan empire, on the principle of agreeing to differ, the ten persecutions would have been reduced by nine, for there would have been nobody left to persecute. It is not without reason, accordingly, that Dr. Döllinger lays down, as an indispensable condition of all negotiations for reunion, the acceptance not only of Holy Scripture, but also of the three œcumenical Creeds, interpreted by the teaching of the ancient Church, before East and West were separated. This was in fact the ground taken, and with perfect success for the moment, at the Council of Florence, though insincerity on both sides, and lust of dominion on one, reduced the agreement to a *fiasco* :

Preface.   xxiii.

and we have a more permanent record of the positive results of such an appeal in the independent but concurrent witness of the dogmatic canons of Trent and the " Orthodox Confession of Faith," sanctioned in 1672 by the Eastern Synod of Bethlehem.[1]

But it would be a grievous mistake to suppose that Protestants alone are interested in the reunion of Christendom, as neither are they alone responsible for its divisions. There are few quarrels, public or private, in which the fault lies wholly on one side, and the Reformation is certainly not one of them. The great ecclesiastical revolution which dates from the ninth century, as it was the immediate occasion of the separation of East and West, became also the remote cause of the schism of the sixteenth century, by giving the first impulse to the new administrative system, which had by that time attained such enormous dimensions. And there was unfortunately much on the Catholic side at that

[1] It is admitted by theologians, on both sides, that the continued quarrel between the Latin and Greek Churches still hinges on the dispute about the primacy, which was its source ; and that if this were amicably settled, the remaining differences, including the question of the *Filioque*, would not be difficult of adjustment. See on this point the testimony of a recent ultramontane writer, Father Tondini, who quotes a dissertation of the learned Belgian Jesuit, De Buck, *Pope of Rome, and Popes of the Oriental Church*, pp. 4, 5 ; and cf. the speech of the Russian deputy, Dr. Ossinin, at the Munich Congress last year.

critical epoch to deepen and embitter the antagonism which had long been growing up, and had left its mark on the Councils, as well as on the literature and religious life, of the fifteenth century. To speak of Tetzel's indulgence-box as the cause of the Reformation, is to confound sign with substance, but it was one of many outward indications of a state of things sure sooner or later to produce an explosion, if it was not remedied. And the remedy of the counter-reformation, besides being partial, came too late. Had all Popes of that age been like-minded with Adrian VI., and all Cardinals such as Contarini and Sadolet, the religious history of the last three centuries might have been a very different one; and the intolerant spirit which helped to create the breach has lived on to keep it open and widen it. We have all, Catholics and Protestants alike, been far too ready to hug ourselves in self-complacent isolation, and too little disposed, in the words of " the profound and pious Möhler," to " stretch a friendly hand to one another, and exclaim, in the consciousness of a common guilt, ' We all have erred; the Church alone cannot err. We all have sinned; the Church alone is spotless.' This *open confession of guilt on both sides,*" adds the author, " will be followed by the festival of reconciliation."[1] And that open confession, which Möhler desiderated forty years ago, is a desideratum still. If Protestants are narrow and unreasonable, and refuse, as they often do, to look an inch beyond the bare letter of the Bible, as interpreted by what they call their private judgment, but what is in reality a mere floating Protestant tradition, Catholics, on the other hand, are apt to content themselves with pointing proudly, almost scornfully, to the unbroken unity of the Church, and telling outsiders to take care of themselves; the loss is theirs alone.

The statement is hardly accurate in the letter, for whenever there has been any serious thought of reconciling East and West, the Popes themselves have always dealt with the Easterns as constituting a portion of the Church, not as mere outsiders. But I do not care to wrangle over niceties of terminology. However we interpret the unity of the Church, the broad fact remains that Christendom is divided. To the outward eye, and as a witness to mankind, the Church is no longer one, as it was in the early ages, as it was in Western Europe up to the sixteenth century. Then,

[1] Möhler's *Symbolism*, Eng. Trans., vol. ii. p. 32, first published in 1832. The passage is quoted in Cardinal Wiseman's *Letter to Lord Shrewsbury*.

like Him who sent her, the divine messenger spoke with authority, for her credentials were visibly written on her regal brow: *incessu patuit dea.* There was one unfailing answer to doubts and difficulties, which was felt to be practically conclusive; and though no one could be better able than St. Augustine to grapple with intellectual error, his most effective argument lay in an appeal to fact; *Securus judicat orbis terrarum.* It is not so now, when the *orbis terrarum* is divided, and the Church's witness is discredited by the discordant clamours of hostile sects. Protestant countries have no monopoly of scepticism. It is as rife, at the very least, in France and Italy as in England. Only the other day a popular French newspaper announced that "Christianity has fatally disorganized civilisation, and its advent may be defined as 'the first invasion of the barbarians.' Now, all the merit of the barbarians was to arrive at the point where there should be no more barbarians: in the same way the advantage of Christianity is to arrive at the point where there will be neither Pagans nor Christians, but freethinkers, *definitely liberated from every God.*"[1] Why has the French Church, with her

[1] *République Française,* quoted in the *Times* of July 15, 1872.

Preface.

vast machinery, her eloquent preachers, her devoted priesthood, so little hold on the male intellect of the country, that public opinion is more than tolerant of Atheism ? Several answers might be given, and indeed have been given, in detail by those best qualified to speak ;[1] but they will be found ultimately to resolve themselves into that one radical evil, which is the fruitful source of such manifold corruption and disease, the disunion of Christendom. To quote the testimony of one of the ablest of our living writers, who cannot certainly be accused of excessive ecclesiastical sympathies : " As things are, rationalism and fatalistic reveries may be laboriously confuted, but amidst the energies and aspirations of a regenerated Christendom they would spontaneously pass away."[2]

The question before us then is one which, apart from all motives of charity for others, Catholics, for their own sakes, cannot afford to ignore. All sections of our distracted Christendom, each in its own way, are

[1] See, *e.g.* a remarkable passage at the close of Father Gratry's *Second Letter to Mgr. Déchamps* (pp. 49, 50), on " the school of error " within the Church, which is the great hindrance to her progress.

[2] Goldwin Smith's *Lectures on the Study of History*, p. 181. The writer had just said, "The reunion of Christendom is likely at last to become a practical aim. Probably it would be a greater service to humanity, on philosophical as well as religious grounds, to contribute the smallest unit towards this consummation, than to construct the most perfect demonstration of the free personality of man."

suffering the penalty of a common sin, and till this is frankly acknowledged on all sides there can be no hope of reconciliation. I have said that an union on the basis of mutual disagreement would be at once useless and impossible, but it is no less unreal to propose an unconditional surrender. He who wills the end must will the means, and those who adopt this tone towards their separated brethren cannot be credited with any sincere desire for that peace which—let us remember—is promised *hominibus bonæ voluntatis.* In fact, as Dr Döllinger has pointed out, there is no greater hindrance to reunion than the line taken on the subject by a powerful party in the Church, which found singularly clear and forcible expression some years ago in a characteristic pronouncement of the *Dublin Review* against an eirenic publication, then recently issued by a devout and learned Catholic layman. "The Church apostolic, undivided, and universal," rejoined his critic, "stands alone among other religious communities, with everything to bestow, nothing to receive." She admits no right to parley with her, "her call, whether to individuals or communities, is a summons not to treat but to surrender. She sits as judge in her own controversy, and the only plea she admits is a *Con-*

fiteor, the only prayer she listens to a *Miserere.*" How far such language breathes the true spirit of the Church or of the Church's Lord, how far it is consistent with the recorded utterances of some of the wisest of her pontiffs and the holiest of her Saints, or with the precedents of former negotiations with external bodies, I do not stay to examine here.[1] Those who are familiar with the facts will have no difficulty in answering the question for themselves. It is enough for my present purpose to observe that such is unhappily the habitual language, and represents the habitual policy, of what Dr. Newman has characterized as an " aggressive, insolent faction," but which just now is tyrannously dominant in the Church.

Let me give but one example of this. Ten years ago, Ketteler, Bishop of Mayence, one of the most influential of the German episcopate, published a work under the title of *Liberty, Authority, and the Church*,[2] which contained the most frank and full confession of the terrible evils resulting both from the earlier rupture between East and West, and from " the no less deplorable division of the Catholic Church

[1] Some remarks on this point will be found in my " Postscript on Catholic Unity," in *Essays on the Reunion of Christendom*. Hayes.

[2] *Freiheit, Autorität und Kirche*, Mainz, 1862.

in the West, which for three centuries has preyed on our vitals, and is the source of such deadly mischief." He urges and conjures all sincere Christians "to pray for the reunion of all the Christian confessions," and " would still more rejoice to see members of different Christian communities deliberate together for the recital of some common prayer,"—exactly, by the way, what was done in England fifteen years ago, and has since been condemned by the Roman Inquisition.[1] The Bishop goes on to say that nearly all the charges brought against the Church spring out of misapprehensions, " and these almost always have their origin in the imperfections and infirmities of members of the Church;" and then he pointedly insists, for the information of Protestants, that the infallibility of the Church "resides only in the whole body of the Episcopate united to the successor of St. Peter, and extends only to truths proclaimed by Christ."[2] The work also contained emphatic assertions of the rights of conscience and the absolute unlawfulness of all religious coercion. It naturally excited considerable attention and very general sympathy in

[1] The A. P. U. C. was founded on the feast of the Nativity of our Lady, 1857, including clergy and laity of the English and Roman Catholic Churches among its first members.

[2] The passage is cited at length in my *Letter to F. Lockhart*, pp. 107-110.

Preface. xxxi

Germany, and was as naturally most unacceptable to the party whose principles it so directly contravened, and who have the ear of Rome. On account of the author's position it was not put on the Index, but it was well understood by himself as well as by others to be implicitly condemned in the Syllabus,[1] and, which is the main point, Bishop Ketteler has found it discreet to adopt an entirely different line on religious questions since then.

So much for the tyrannous influence of the dominant faction. That their attitude towards external communions, which recognises nothing but a "*Confiteor* and a *Miserere*," must prove, as it always has proved, absolutely fatal, so far as it extends, to the very idea of conciliation, is obvious on the face of it, and must be perfectly obvious to themselves. Not such was the attitude or the spirit of Leander, Sancta Clara, and Panzani, of Bossuet or Spinola, of Adrian VI., Urban VIII., Innocent XI., Clement XIV.; and only by proceeding in a spirit the very opposite of this can the wounds of Christendom be healed. There have been many on all

[1] He attempted indeed in a subsequent pamphlet, *Deutschland nach dem Kriege* (1867), to explain away the force of the implied censure by the strange hypothesis, that the articles of the Syllabus did not contain a general principle, but only applied to particular countries!

sides, Catholics, Anglicans, Lutherans, in former days as now, who have laboured and longed for that blessed consummation, and have not lived to see it; some, like Spinola and Leibnitz, in one generation, Du Pin and Wake in another, whose names are indelibly associated with the sacred cause. And in almost every case the fairest hopes have been wrecked, not on a religious, but a political difficulty, as seems only too likely to be the case with the present unionistic movement in the East, to which Dr Döllinger has referred. What the good Bishop Doyle said of one such attempt is more or less true of all or nearly all: "its failure was owing more to Princes than to Priests, more to State policy than to a difference of belief." How true are the concluding words of the same letter: "They are pride and points of honour which keep us divided on many subjects, not a love of Christian humility, charity, and truth!"[1]

And there are many more, of every clime and age, in remote English villages, in the seclusion of foreign convents, in the privacy of domestic life, before gleaming altars, on lingering death-beds, who have watched, and toiled, and prayed for the dawn of that

[1] Letter to Lord Ripon (1824), published in Fitzpatrick's *Life, Times, and Correspondence of Dr. Doyle*, pp. 421 *sqq.*, and in *Union Review*, vol. i. pp. 12 *sqq.*

Preface.

second Pentecost, who are praying for it still in the brightness of the everlasting sunshine, whose names we know not, and shall never know on earth, over whose forgotten graves their guardian angels whisper that most musical of all the Beatitudes, *Beati pacifici, quoniam filii Dei vocabuntur.* There are many yet among us who are striving and praying for it now. And besides all these there is a vast multitude of intercessors, whom no man can number, of every kindred, tribe, and tongue, sunflushed with the glory of the Uncreated Vision, and gazing on the pure reflection of unsullied truth that is mirrored for ever and for ever on the waveless surface of the crystal sea, whose sight is purged from all earthly film and their souls from taint of human passion, who cease not day and night to cry continually, "How long, O Lord, how long?" And we, too, if we really cared about the matter, should make it a subject of definite contemplation, definite action, definite, united, persevering, pertinacious prayer. We should, in the startling language of Scripture, "weary" the Supreme Judge with our importunities;[1] we should interest all the glorified host in

---

[1] The original word (in Luke xviii. 5), ὑπωπιάζῃ (*Vulg.* "sugillet") is far stronger, and will hardly indeed bear literal translation. A more tre-

our supplications to the Most High. *Omnes Sancti et Sanctæ Dei, intercedite pro nobis!*

And to all who, in whatever communion, and under whatever form, worship in sincerity our common Lord, I would say, Do not put from you the suggestion as unpractical, or trivial, or inopportune, as a morbid craving for the satisfaction of an ideal want. A craving which is rooted in the deepest instincts of our moral nature, and is strengthened by menacing phenomena in the present condition of society, whose accumulated weight presses more heavily each day on the intellect and conscience, is no mere sickly dream; and a divine ideal can never be impossible of attainment. If we have come to look on religious disunion as a chronic and tolerable evil, or even—and there are some who seem so to view it—as a positive advantage, that is only because long use has inured us to a state of things which ought to be intolerable to Christians, as it has long been the palmary argument and impregnable stronghold of the mocking enemies of Christ. "Go ye, make disciples of all nations, baptizing them," was the original commission of the Church, and now, at the end of eighteen centuries of missionary enterprise,

mendous assertion of the duty and efficacy of prayer it would be impossible to conceive.

and when every heathen land has been incarnadined in martyr-blood, three-fourths of mankind are unbaptized! "That they may all be one, even as We are One, that the world may believe that Thou hast sent Me," was the Redeemer's dying intercession for His followers; and now, in this nineteenth century since His Crucifixion, there are more Christians sects in England alone than there were believers in the Upper Room at Jerusalem after the Ascension! And what is the upshot? Simply this, that every shred of the revelation He committed to His Church is openly disputed by those who profess to be His disciples, while the great mass of the poor, to whom especially the Gospel was to be preached, are left to live the life and die the death of heathen in a nominally Christian land, because those who should have taught them His word and ministered His sacraments have wasted their energies, and lost half their faith and all their authority, in perpetual bickerings with one another as to what that word and those sacraments are. Truly, if Christianity be a divine revelation, and the Christian Church is to be its teacher, the religious outcome of the last three centuries of division is a spectacle to make infidels triumph and angels weep.

But anyhow the case is hopeless, and it will be our wisdom to acquiesce quietly in the inevitable : reunion is an idle dream. Why ? *Simply because we choose to make it so.* There is a story of a farmer in a country parish, who was consulted by the rector, after a dry season, as to whether he should use the prayer for rain. " Well, sir," was the reply, " there is no use in your praying for rain while the wind continues in the north." We have acted for three centuries and more in the spirit of that pious and intelligent rustic, and during all that period the theological wind has set very steadily from the north. As long as we continue to emulate his example, we have only ourselves to thank if it should blow from the same quarter for the next three centuries. We have not, because we ask not ; we ask, and have not, because we ask amiss. Too many of us do not ask at all. Like the gods of Epicurus, " they lie beside their nectar," and regard the religious condition of the world, if they ever think about it, much as the deity of a certain school of modern thinkers is supposed to contemplate, if he ever does contemplate, the universe he created, if indeed he did create it, — with an otiose if not cynical detachment. Reunion, they say, would be a miracle, and to pray for miracles is idle, if not presumptuous. And many, who would shrink from the virtual atheism of such an avowal, are unreal when they pray for unity, because their normal standard of conduct and opinion is in direct contradiction with their prayers; out of the same mouth proceeds blessing and cursing. If there is truth in the proverb, *Qui laborat orat*, if it is unreal to ask for what we will make no efforts to attain, still less can we expect our petitions to be heard, if we do all in our power to thwart them. While we habitually feel and act on the tacit assumption that our divisions are irreconcileable, that all the right is on one side, and the sole legitimate object of discussion is not peace, but victory; while we are eager to incriminate and slow to explain, resolved to learn nothing and forget nothing, to admit no faults on our own side, and condone none on the other; while we are never weary of flinging at each other's heads the fagots of Smithfield and the gibbets of Tyburn, like schoolboys in a snowball match,—so long we are doing our utmost to create the impossibility we affect to deplore. Far better let the dead bury their dead, and, while we respect the constancy of the sufferers on either side, not seek to make controversial capital out of past atrocities, which disgraced religion; still less, as some would have us, desire to emulate them. Mary and her evil counsellors did more, no doubt, than all the Reformers put together, to brand the tradition of Protestant exclusiveness into the heart and conscience of England; and we, if we are wise, shall take warning by their example, how unity can never be restored.[1] Actual persecution is, of course, out of the question in the present state of society, but

[1] It is impossible to condemn too strongly the Marian burnings, whether on grounds of principle or of policy. But it is fair to remember that the sufferers never shrank from inflicting the penalties they were ready to endure bravely, when their turn came: they had no difference with their persecutors about the principle, but only about its application. Cranmer, of course, I put out of the reckoning altogether. It may or may not be true that he held the fingers of the peevish boy in whose name he misruled England, while forcing him to sign the death-warrant of a visionary little less orthodox and infinitely more honest than himself; but anyhow he was no more a genuine persecutor than a genuine martyr. He burnt impugners of the Real Presence as long as it suited his interests, and he was burnt for denying it—probably with sincerity, for his range of belief seems to have been a limited one—after he had solemnly recanted his denial. But Latimer, who was a typical Reformer and unquestionably honest, preached a sermon worthy of Torquemada, while Prior Forest was being roasted to death over a slow fire for denying the spiritual supremacy of Henry VIII. And I am afraid there can be no doubt that Elizabeth's Jesuit victims would have been equally ready to burn any one who denied the spiritual or temporal supremacy of the Pope. "The toleration of heresy," says Sir J. Mackintosh, "was deemed by men of all persuasions to be as unreasonable as it would now be thought to propose the impunity of murder." For copious authorities on the Protestant side, see a remarkable article on "The Protestant Theory of Persecution" in the *Rambler* for March 1862.

the persecuting temper can express itself in a hundred ways, and is the precise contradictory of that temper in which alone we can meet our alienated fellow-Christians with any prospect of ultimate agreement.

And never surely was the obligation more urgent, never was there more in the circumstances of the day to supply both warning and encouragement, than now. Ours is in one sense a peculiarly religious age. Religious questionings, aspirations, doubts, interpenetrate its literature and thought, trouble its policy, and mingle in the details of its social life. It organizes religious meetings, congresses, and synods of every hue. The religious question, as it has been said, is the order of the day. And this is a ground of encouragement. On the other hand, it is also a very irreligious age. Scepticism has never before been so open-mouthed, so widespread, and withal so oppressively respectable as it has recently become. Its apostles do not scruple to assure us, with an engaging frankness, that virtue and vice are "natural products in the same sense as sugar and vitriol," or that prayer is an obsolete superstition to be classed with the belief in " witches, dreams, astrology, and auguries of good or evil luck," for which the civilized world will learn to substitute the equally "ennobling" and "consoling" contemplation of the "solidarity between themselves and what surrounds them through the endless reactions of physical laws." But still it is not the mocking scepticism of Tom Paine or Voltaire. It is sedate, refined, decorous, respectable; it sometimes almost seems to be devout. But if we are tempted to let ourselves imagine that in losing its grossness it has lost its sting, we are likely to be cruelly undeceived. And indeed already there are not wanting ominous signs of the spirit which deluged the Colosseum with Christian blood, or voices among those which would banish the "pale Galilean" from an emancipated world, that do not suffer us to forget in what guise the goddess Reason was enthroned, not a century ago, on the high altar of Notre Dame.

Such moral and intellectual aberrations will never be disposed of by mere force of reasoning, however laborious and acute. They thrive in the cold shade of our mutual hatreds, and would fade away like a noisome exhalation in the bracing atmosphere and clear strong sunshine of a Christendom at unity with itself. But if there still remains "the little rift within the lute," if the trumpet still gives an uncertain sound, when it summons us to the battle with Antichrist,—and the spirit of Antichrist is rife among us now—how shall his assault be met by the disjointed and spasmodic efforts of a straggling multitude, without leader, discipline, or common watchword? But it is the glory of Divine Providence to bring good out of evil, and the infidel aggression, which threatens us on every side, may well be His predestined instrument for reuniting Christian believers in presence of a common foe.

On the special bearing of the Reunion question on the Established Church I will make but one remark here. The present agitation against the Athanasian Creed, and the official relations of the clergy to a legislature which has already sanctioned adultery, and is only too likely ere long to sanction incest, must have brought home two facts very distinctly to the minds even of its most attached and loyal adherents. In the first place, they cannot fail to perceive in what a difficult position an isolated communion finds itself, whatever may be pleaded in defence or excuse of its isolation, when called upon to vindicate the most elementary principles of Christian morality and belief.[1] And,

[1] By the present law a clergyman is bound, on application, to allow the

secondly, these difficulties afford a fresh illustration of the insecure tenure on which the Establishment, as such, holds its ground.[1] And disestablishment, whenever it comes, while leaving the Church more free to negotiate with external bodies, will also make the need for external support more urgent, by withdrawing the prestige and cohesive power supplied by union with the State.

And now, I am afraid I have detained the reader too long, if indeed he has allowed himself to be detained, from studying testimony far weightier and more authoritative than any I could hope to give. It is in itself a remarkable fact, that "the venerable Nestor of Catholic theology," as he has been styled, whose life has been spent as a Catholic professor and prelate in the very centre of northern Catholicism, and who has himself, in former days, devoted the vast resources of his intellect and learning to the exposure

---

use of his church for the re-marriage (so-called) of a divorced parishioner, whether guilty of previous adultery or not, and may be compelled to marry the "innocent party" himself; every such pretended marriage being of course a nullity and a sacrilege. A notorious case occurred not long ago in one of the principal parish churches of London.

[1] This is expressly recognised in Dr. Pusey's letter on the subject, published in the *Times* of Aug. 13.

Preface. xliii

of Protestant error,[1] should, during the last twelve years, have scarcely published a single work without pointedly introducing this question of Reunion, which he has now, when ultramontanism has just won its crowning triumph, set himself expressly to discuss. Speaking from the platform of a long experience, a profound acquaintance with the past history of the Church, and an extensive familiarity with the present condition of both Catholic and Protestant society, he declares that union to be at once a supreme necessity of the Christian commonwealth and a perfectly practicable achievement. It is not the voice of a youthful zealot, or a dreaming mystic, or a fiery reformer, which addresses us, but a venerable priest, full of years and of honours, cautious by temperament, and of a nation pre-eminent for its critical acumen, conservative and Catholic to the backbone in his instincts and habits, who sums up in these weighty words the concentrated convictions of a lifetime. It is indeed the utterance of a *mitis sapientia*, chastened by long years of toil and trial, but also of an enthusiasm, in the best and truest sense of the word,

[1] See, *e.g.* his *Die Reformation* in 3 vols. and his *Martin Luther*.

which only shines out with brighter lustre through the veil of patient suffering and advancing age, because it is based on the faith of an unerring promise, and lives in the habitual vision of the world beyond the grave.

H. N. O.

Feast of the Nativity of our Lady, 1872.

LECTURE I.

GENERAL REVIEW OF THE RELIGIOUS CONDITION OF THE WORLD.

THE Christian portion of the human family may be reckoned at some 350 million souls, and includes about thirty per cent. of the inhabitants of the world. But Christians are divided into many larger or smaller communities or churches, which mutually exclude each other, allowing no communion of worship, sacraments, or prayer, and accusing one another of errors or departures from the teaching of Christ so serious as to endanger salvation.

Divisions and formations of separate churches were not indeed infrequent during the first thousand years after Christ. But they were generally of short duration, and after a while were reabsorbed into the great Catholic Church. So it was with the Churches which took their rise from the Arian controversies, and those which had separated mainly on ethical grounds, referring to ecclesiastical discipline, such as the Novatians, Donatists, Montanists, and most of the Western sects. But this cannot be said of the separations and newly formed communities of the last thousand years. These still continue, that is, the principal parties or churches, with, on the whole, no diminution of vital and expansive power. Let us take a bird's-eye view of them.

The Greek Catholic or Eastern Church, which numbers about seventy-five million members, in Russia, Turkey, and Greece, has separated from the Roman Catholic, or Western Church, which contains about 180 millions. This separation began about the middle of the eleventh century, but was only consummated in the thirteenth, in consequence of the taking of Constantinople and violent subjugation of the Greeks by Westerns acting under papal inspiration. To this Church, which takes the name of "Orthodox," are closely related the Nestorians, the remnant of a Church once widely spread in the interior of Asia, which has been separated from the rest of the Christian world since the middle of the fifth century, in consequence of the controversies about the Person of Christ, and the Monophysites, who separated about the same time, and from similar causes, as representatives of the opposite

Religious Condition of the World. 3

view, and formed a far more numerous body than the Nestorians, comprising three national Churches, the Armenian, the Coptic in Egypt, and the Abyssinian.

And as the Church has been separated since the twelfth century into two numerically unequal halves, each going its own way and accusing the other of schism and heresy, so in the sixteenth century came the great split in the Western or Latin Church, which cut far deeper. Out of the reforming movement which after 1517 took possession of the whole populace of Western Europe, sprang by degrees new ecclesiastical societies, which are generically termed Protestant. And hence three great systems have grown up. There is first the Lutheran, covering Germany, Scandinavia, and the eastern coasts of Russia, about thirty millions strong; then the Reformed, including some twelve million inhabitants of Switzerland, the Netherlands, Scotland, and parts of Germany and Hungary. Distinguished from both these is the English Episcopal Church, still as yet the State Church, which has kept closer in its constitution and worship to the two ancient Churches of the East and West, and from the comparative brevity and vagueness of the Thirty-nine Articles which form its doctrinal confession, is on the one hand less widely removed from Catholic dogmas, while on the other it allows more room for differences of teaching and interpretation.

Meanwhile, besides these great national Churches there sprang up at and after the time of the Reformation many smaller sects, which, though several have died out, not only still survive—chiefly in England and North America—but are constantly being increased in number. There are at present about a hundred of these smaller religious communities, numbering some 18,000 members. Many of them have never extended beyond the land of their birth, and are hardly known by name elsewhere. Others, especially the Anabaptists, count their adherents by millions. Nor are these sects always based on doctrinal distinctions. Sometimes peculiarities in social arrangements or worship, or methods of education and individual culture, form the leading characteristic, as is shown in the case of the Moravians and the English and American Methodists. It is chiefly in the Anglo-Saxon race, in both its English and American branches, that the capacity and inclination for forming sects has developed itself, while the German people, if we except the Swabian branch, has never manifested such a tendency.

The circle of thought within which most of these sects revolve is a very narrow one, and the differences are often confined to points of infinitesimal importance. Not unfrequently jealousy or love of notoriety, or even a financial speculation, is the inspiring motive of the founders of a new sect; but the mere fact of their so often succeeding proves how ready the people are to welcome such associations.

It is true that smaller communities are sometimes distinguished by a stricter discipline and higher code of morality, for the individual is more supported and upheld by the body of which he is a member, more closely watched and far more dependent on the good opinion of the rest. This moral earnestness, and abstinence at least from ordinary vices, is generally, *e.g.*, to be observed in the Anabaptist settlements, and their example benefits the members of other bodies also.

Many of these little communities may exist for centuries without either injuring or profiting the rest of the world. They lead a quiet life, far from the busy throng of men, sometimes closely hemmed in by the adherents of antagonistic creeds, and thus, as it were, welded together, or perhaps united also by ties of blood. And so they maintain themselves with indestructible vigour in spite of constant dangers and ill-treatment. In this way the Nestorians or Christians of St. Thomas have now existed for 1300 years in East India, and the Copts still longer in Egypt.

We thus find two principal families of Christian Churches,—first the ancient Churches, whose continuity has never been interrupted, and which reach up by a regular succession to the first beginnings of Christianity, however great may have been their internal changes; such are the Eastern Church with its daughters, the Russian, Armenian, Coptic, and Nestorian; and the Western Catholic Church. The other family is composed of those Churches which have issued directly or indirectly from that powerful religious movement called the Reformation, and the communities and sects which have again broken off from them.

This great number of divisions and separate Churches has its good as well as its evil consequences, but we shall have no doubt on a closer inspection as to which preponderate. As to the first, it may be said that every new sect or Church is an experiment, or a trial of certain doctrines or usages and regulations peculiar to the sect. Here Gamaliel's maxim may be applied, and Church history regarded as a great course of experiments; what has held its own, or even increased in strength with the lapse of time, has conquered for itself the right of permanence, while what passes away and disappears under the stream was not worth preserving. But then history and experience contradict this view. Islam, which must be considered at bottom a Christian heresy, the bastard offspring of a Christian father and Jewish mother, and is indeed more closely allied to Christianity than Manicheeism, which is reckoned a Christian sect,—Islam has now maintained for 1250 years an at least outwardly unshaken dominion over a large portion of mankind, 120 millions, and moreover still makes fresh advances every year in Africa, Australia, and the interior of India, which exceed the progress of Christianity in those countries. It has made large encroachments on Christianity, from which it has alienated whole regions, without, on the other hand, suffering any important losses through conversion to our faith. And yet how clear it is to us that history has already pronounced sentence on this religion, and sealed its rejection, when we consider the once flourishing, now fallen, condition of those lands where Islam prevails, and of their denizens. Such are Asia Minor,

Syria, Persia, Cyprus, Egypt, and a closer inspection proves that it is precisely to their false religion that their unhappy condition and gradual decay and extinction are due. Nor is this at all inconsistent with the fact that the same religion has benefited peoples in a lower stage of development, as has been recently observed in the case of negroes converted to Mahometanism in South Africa.

It cannot be denied that there is something repulsive in the present aspect of the Christian world, with its sharply-divided and hostile Churches and sects, mutually hating and incriminating one another. And were we not accustomed to the sight from our youth up, it would strike us as still uglier, and the contrast between the idea and the reality would be more glaring in our eyes. In all the other highest departments of life, in science, in art, the power of attraction and union of minds asserts itself, and sooner or later dissonance and hatred are lost in harmony. With religion alone it is different; what according to its inmost essence was meant to be the most powerful bond of union, because possessed and filled with love, has been the cause of so many divisions—what was to establish peace has kindled strife and bloody wars—what was to give men

Religious Condition of the World.

certainty and confidence has provoked doubt and planted mistrust in their minds. The division of the two great ancient Churches of East and West is, or rather was, unmeaning, because of their essential unity of doctrine; now, on the other hand, since July 18, 1870, it is different. And here permit me to observe how perilous may be the consequences of this ecclesiastical division in the immediate future.

There can be no question that, since the end of the Franco-German war, the Eastern question is the weightiest, and at all events far the most difficult, question of the day. Considered from a purely political point of view, it must be called simply insoluble; and yet on its solution hinges the future of Austria, and in no slight degree of the world generally, which has now to take in the German Empire. No doubt time might eventually bring a solution, but only in the distant future; for the Turkish people, which now tyrannizes over millions of Christians, is, so to speak, at the point of death; it decreases considerably every year, while the Christians steadily increase. But the situation is too intolerable, and the impatience of mankind too great, to wait for the solution of time, and the great crisis is constantly forcing its way to the front.

Russians and Greeks—the great majority, that is, of the population of the Empire—are co-religionists, members of the same Church. Will Russia be willing or able to look on quietly much longer on a situation such as all correspondents on the spot describe it to be, which no diplomatic intervention can touch, because it is grounded in the very nature of things, inasmuch as for the Mahometan conscience there is no rule but the Koran, which breathes only hatred and contempt for Christians? And thus all the efforts of England, France, and Austria to avert the catastrophe have as yet been fruitless, except for gaining time. Russia alone holds the keys of the destiny of the Turkish Empire. And who will contradict Russia if she decides that it is a duty to be carried out by force of arms, to improve the desperate condition of the Christians in that Empire? Have not all the European powers acted from time to time on this principle? But if only an ecclesiastical union between East and West were brought about, how completely would the whole situation be changed! A general co-operation of the great Christian powers would then become possible for warding off the danger from both the Austrian and German Empires, and a solution in accordance with the balance of power in Europe might be found. More than that: slight as is the real difference between the Russo-Greek and Latin Churches, the Russian people are profoundly impressed with the belief, long since studiously fostered by their rulers, that theirs is the sole true and legitimate Church, and all foreign nations are to be regarded as heretical and unbelieving, and that consequently every foreign war is a religious war of believers against unbelievers. It will be remembered by what means the Emperor Nicholas sought to increase and accentuate this national prejudice. His proclamation of March 26, 1848, is well known: "Hear and bow down, ye Gentiles, for God is with us;" and his speech to the Russian and Polish Bishops, on May 26, 1849: "The true faith survives in Russia only; in the West it is utterly lost." The Czar Alexander II., also, after his accession, addressed the army as "the true soldiers and champions of the Church, the throne, and the fatherland"—so that the Russian soldier is inspired by the belief that his first duty is to defend the Church with his arms. It is obvious what a lever this view supplies, and what an enthusiasm it may kindle in war, and how grave would be the danger for Germany if ever an anti-German or Panslavist party succeeded in involving the colossal Empire in a war with us, and this war came to be considered by Russia as a religious war.

On the other hand, the Churches which sprang from the Reformation of the sixteenth century have been gradually, and for the most part reluctantly, urged or violently driven into separation by profound differences of doctrine, and when once all intercommunion had been entirely broken off, the original differences of doctrine grew wider, and were moulded into systems whose hard inflexible letter made all reconciliation impossible. Historically considered, we know that the Reformation was inevitable, and that, when no room was allowed it in the bosom of the ancient Church, a breach of unity was the necessary consequence. Nor can we blind ourselves to the fact that it has had many beneficial results, and has in various ways proved a gain even to the ancient Church which was so hostile to it. We see that it has created a rich intellectual world, and given an impulse to every form of mental activity. It has become the most powerful and permanent force in modern history. But the three centuries and a half of its existence have apparently sufficed to bring out and mature whatever spiritual resources it contained within itself. That period has also supplied evidence that these new ecclesiastical creations have faults and defects of their own which they have no inherent power of remedying, and that they are incapable of really and permanently satisfying all the religious needs of mankind. The morbid hankering after division, the discontent of individuals, the incompetence to form any church organizations standing firmly on their own foundations, have long been sensibly felt; and it is impossible not to perceive that in the first heat of the struggle and passionate excitement of the Reformation tempest, many doctrines and practices of the ancient Church were much too hastily rejected, leaving a gap it is difficult to fill up. The time will come, and in the opinion and desire of many is already come, when the Petrine and Pauline Churches will develope into a Johannean Church, or, as used to be said in mediæval times, to the period of the Father and the Son will succeed the age of the Holy Ghost. And this would be brought about by the existing Churches being content to learn and receive of one another, and to impart to one another their peculiar possessions and privileges, and thus enter into the noblest community of goods, but above all, by their setting a higher price on the doctrines and creeds which they have inherited and confess in common than on what divides them. Many will ask whether this is possible. I reply that it must be possible, for it is a duty. No doubt a great purification and renewal of the Church in the sixteenth century was a pressing need : the condition of things had become untenable and intolerable. But this process might have been accomplished without the divisions which grew out of it, whereas not only have the Catholics separated from the Protestants, but among these last, the Lutherans have separated from the Reformed (Calvinists), and the Anglicans from both alike. In this then we must acknowledge a grievous fault of men, originating in their passions and sinful errors, as history abundantly testifies. On that point all schools and parties are substantially agreed, only that each throws the whole blame, or the greater part of it, on its opponents. Every Church maintains that the rest are bound to unite with it, and thus atone for the crime of their forefathers.

That Christ, the Founder of the Church, desired and enjoined its unity is clear. In His Eucharistic prayer we read, " That they all may be one ; that as Thou, Father, art in Me and I in Thee, they also may be one in

Us, that the world may believe that Thou hast sent Me."[1]
Nay, this unity is, as He further prays, to be a perfect one, and therefore the most penetrating and purest conceivable among men. And here it is especially to be noted that this unity of Christian believers is itself to serve as the means to a further end; it is to be a testimony for the world in general, and for all nations, of the truth and divinity of the teaching of Christ. And such it was in the early ages. " See how these Christians love one another," was then a common saying of the heathen. According to the will of our Lord, men ought always to be able to say, " A religion which unites its adherents, and holds together a vast society so closely, without any coercion, through the Spirit which animates it, bears the impress of its truth and divinity." And thereby He has of course given us to understand that ecclesiastical divisions and a multiplicity of separate Churches will produce just the opposite impression on non-Christian nations, and on many Christians too, and will be to them a great stumblingblock and occasion of serious doubt as to the truth of Christianity. Any one who wishes to realize this has only to ask some educated Jew resident among us what impression the strife and controversy of the Churches makes upon him.

[1] John xvii. 21.

At the same time, no Church can ignore the command and commission to teach and baptize heathen nations. It is a duty and mission laid upon us to bring within the reach of foreign nations the benefits of civilisation, culture, moral improvement, and elevation of both family and civil life, by the only possible means, of religious instruction and ecclesiastical organization, whereby we ourselves obtained them. But more than two-thirds of the inhabitants of the world are heathen; there are still 800 million souls unconverted to Christianity. And yet we may truly say that almost the whole human race is possessed with a feeling of restlessness unknown even in the ages of the great migration of nations, while at the same time the wonderfully increased facilities of intercourse have roused a passion for travel, and an irresistible impulse to more intimate union among different peoples. The most remote, obscure, and unknown corners of the earth are explored, all the laboriously constructed barriers of earlier days give way to pressure from without, or are torn down by the nations which erected them, and we observe with surprise, in how many parts of the earth civilized men and barbarians, Christians and heathen, jostle one another, so that in America Chinese meet and mingle with Europeans. We see how nations which have long remained sunk in the lowest depth of moral or intellectual stagnation, are suddenly drawn into the vortex of the great world-stream which has broken in upon them. It seems as though no nation of the world was to be allowed any longer to go on vegetating independently on its old foundations. Even the great civilized nations of Eastern Asia, the Hindus, the Chinese, the Japanese, are constrained to enter into European conditions and requirements, and to appropriate the arts and methods of education of the Christian West. But this picture, which I have only indicated by a few touches here, while on the one side it encourages the brightest hopes, discloses on the other some dark spots. The first is the fact, more and more forcing itself on the notice of observers, that many of the peoples now dwelling on the earth are not only incapable of any historical existence, but are inevitably doomed to destruction, and are, some slowly, some rapidly, fading away. The Indians in North and South America, the negroes in Australia, the inhabitants of the South Sea Islands, the Hottentots in South Africa, and other tribes, are disappearing. Of the once numerous tribes of North America, many are already extinct, and their very names forgotten. The most harmless contact with strangers, or the mere presence of Europeans or their descendants, is enough to bring havoc on many of the native races.

The study of geography has revealed a yet darker side in the present condition of the nations. Nature herself, the very soil, groans under the burden and curse of a false religion,—for when the people degenerate, nature herself grows brutalized and depraved. The earth is given men to till, but irreligious or misbelieving populations destroy instead of cultivating it; under their hands it becomes unfruitful, and loses its grace and vegetation. Towns and villages decay, and gradually perish, and where once was a rich country and busy population, there is a howling wilderness. No land under Moslem rule can now be called a flourishing one. In the region between the Tigris and Euphrates, the ancient Chaldea, the cradle of the human race, there is a widespread desolation, little agriculture, only a few decayed and impoverished towns, no villages, and a mere roving population, who know nothing of their ancestors, and sink deeper every year into a state of utter barbarism. All those fair and populous cities of which history tells, that vast, civilized and flourishing population which held its place there far into the middle ages, have disappeared, and if the

Religious Condition of the World. 19

reason is asked, there is but one reply—It is the work of a false religion! What a spectacle is presented now by the once great and powerful Persian Empire, a country more than twice the size of Germany, but with only some five million inhabitants, with few towns, and none of which whole quarters are not in ruins, pillaged by a wretched despotic government, and now lying helpless under the assault of a deadly famine, while it feebly awaits the hour when Russia may please to take it in hand.[1] And yet the very religion which exhibits these phenomena in Turkey, North Africa, and Egypt, and which one might suppose to be gradually dying out through the decay of the peoples who are under its curse, shows itself elsewhere full of youthful vigour and elasticity. In the Indian Archipelago and the interior of Africa, from the Niger to the Cape, it is in rapid advance, conquering whole heathen kingdoms in its course, and makes progress even among the Christian Abyssinians. But unfortunately there is no other religion which has so deeply-rooted a hatred to Christianity as Mahometanism, and this hatred is engrained into every nation which embraces it.

[1] [As regards the hollow and unprogressive character of Turkish civilisation, cf. Newman's *Lectures on the Turks*, Lect. iv. "Barbarism and Civilisation."]

LECTURE II.

THE DUTY OF CHRISTIAN NATIONS TO THE HEATHEN, AND ITS GREAT HINDRANCE.

WE are met here by an objection which requires to be disposed of. I will state it in the words of a high authority on the subject of ethnology: "Do not deceive yourselves; every nation has *its own* religion. Catholicity was and is impossible. The German, the Italian, and the Greek have and always had different religions, because they are different nations. We should not speak of Christianity so much as of Christian nations, and of each of these in particular, for it is the national mind which really apprehends and interprets the message according to its capacity." It is true that the author of this passage belongs to a people with whom religion and nationality are so completely identified that the one covers and sustains the other, and neither can exist apart. But his view is contradicted

Duty to the Heathen and its Hindrance.

by the whole course of Christian history, and not only Christianity but Mahometanism has the character of a world-wide religion, destined to embrace many and diverse nationalities. Turks, Arabians, and Persians are as unlike each other as any three nations on about the same level of civilisation well can be, and yet all these have the same religion; and are not the Scotch and Swiss Protestants of wholly different nationality though they have the same religion? There is only so much truth in the view in question, that, in the first place, there are nations whose moral and spiritual condition is so deplorably low, that they have no aptitude for a spiritual religion like the Christian. Such, for instance, are the Papuas of New Holland, those most wretched and apparently most hopelessly degraded of human beings, on whom the labours of missionaries for long years have been wasted. It is true, secondly, that a religion which has once got possession of a nation interpenetrates, and in a sense transforms, the national character, and thus no doubt brings out differences, the cause of which might be confounded with the effect, if it were to be deduced from the original character of the people, whereas it is really the result of a religious faith received from without. It must further be admitted, that however close the similarity of views and Church organization, the apprehension and practice of a religion will vary widely according to national temperament, and these differences will not be removed or equalized by the mere fact of two nations belonging to the same great Church. Thus, for instance, a German Catholic, suddenly transported to Calabria, and master of the language, would find it difficult to realize that he and his neighbours possessed the same religion, so strange would the materialistic and magical distortion of Christianity appear to him. When, again, he first came in contact with the religious notions and practices of a baptized Indian in South America, what violence would he have to do to his feelings before he could realize that they both professed the same faith; while, on the other hand a married pair in Germany, of whom one is a believing Catholic and the other a believing Protestant, can carry on domestic worship and Bible-reading together for years in perfect harmony.

It cannot then be denied that the great Christian powers have a call and a duty to extend to the heathen nations under their dominion, or within the sphere of their influence, the benefits of civilisation. For even those nations which are really cultivated, and possess a literature, art, and a kind of civilisation of their own, such as the Chinese and Japanese, are not, properly speaking, civilized, for they want that humanizing which a morality based on the laws of righteousness and love to man can alone supply, and that depends on religion. There is therefore only one kind of civilisation, which is the product of the Christian spirit, and those nations alone possess a genuine civilisation which have passed under the discipline of the Christian Church, and are still learning in that school. The antithesis to this is barbarism; and it is no paradox, but a notorious fact, that cultivated nations such as those named just now are at the same time barbarous. Even in the bosom of Christian civilisation there must be a constant struggle against the symptoms threatening, either from above or below, a relapse into barbarism. The gravity of the danger has just been exemplified in the frightful tragedy of the Paris Commune, and what is connected with it all over Europe. And therefore what has been called the internal or domestic mission of Europe must be as carefully attended to as the external mission to the heathen; indeed, the former is the more pressing and indispensable of the two.

But here I must explain more precisely what I understand by civilisation, and what I mean by the duty incumbent on the great Christian states and nations, first towards themselves, and then towards the heathen world. Our whole social order, every public and private institution or mode of life, rests, or should rest, on the following truths :—Before God all men are equal, all are called to the highest attainable moral and spiritual perfection, and thence to happiness, and all should love one another as brothers; there should be no castes and no slavery. Every man is a free person, not to be treated as a means or a thing, but as an end in himself. There must therefore be a free development and expression of all powers and capabilities, and legal right of exercising them, limited by due regard for the common liberty of all. Marriage is an institution consecrated by religion on the basis of monogamy and the equal rights of the wife. The father's right over his children is limited and controlled by society, whence child-murder is prohibited, and the State compels parents to provide for the training and education of their children. Labour and chastity are recognised as moral and religious duties, and the relation of the civil power to its subjects as consecrated by religion, so that obedience to law, and lawful authority as ordained by God, becomes a duty, as it is also a duty for authority to keep within lawful limits, without arbitrary caprice or tyranny.

It is the contrary of these ideas and conditions which meets us everywhere in the non-Christian world, whether Buddhist, Brahminical, or Mahometan. Above all, there is everywhere child-murder, especially of female children, and that too practised by the mothers themselves. The woman is a being of lower grade, so that throughout the East it is commonly supposed that only men have souls, and accordingly women are oppressed, maltreated, shut out from all means of education, bought and sold like merchandise, and surrendered to the arbitrary caprice of men like slaves or beasts of burden; and thence comes the system of polygamy, so fatal wherever it is tolerated, and the dissolution of family life which is inseparable from it. Everywhere, too, a disesteem of human life prevails, which is often wantonly lavished to a frightful extent.

It is an oppressive thought that from four to five hundred millions belong to a religion like the Buddhist, which connects with the doctrine of transmigration of souls that of the "Nirvana," holding forth to man as his supreme end a condition of passive and otiose unconsciousness, and commending to him, as the truest and highest virtue, the negation of activity, will, desire, or thought. And where Buddhism ends Brahminism begins, in whose meshes are held between 130 and 140 million Hindus. Here we have a gross Pantheism, with a worship that takes the form of the most indiscriminate idolatry; the crudest arrogance and presumption in the Brahmins, combined with the utmost contempt of man in the case of the lower castes. A cow is more honoured than a Sudra, and a Pariah can be murdered with impunity; there are no rights of man, but only of caste.

And now let us take a glance at those nations whose position in the world entails on them the care of the portion of mankind which stands in grievous need of help. There is England, whose empire on the Ganges has been established for a century, and now embraces all Hindustan, which on the whole rules with a wisdom, justice, and clemency of which history records few examples. There is Russia, whose giant arms embrace the whole of Northern, Western, and Eastern Asia; and France, to which Northern Africa belongs. And what happened to England in the East Indies is happening to both of them: they will be driven on from conquest to conquest.

Russia especially cannot stand still; she must become more and more the arbiter of the destiny of North and Middle Asia. Does she possess the capacities for doing justice to this mission, the greatest and most difficult which can be imposed on any nation or state? England has proved her capacity; Russia is still at the beginning of the great work assigned to her, and has to show that she is equal to the task, and understands not only how to conquer, but how to rule and civilize. Is it not above all requisite that the Russian Church should recognise in the overwhelming duties which are more and more pressing upon her every day, a motive for abandoning her old exclusiveness, and seeking, through union with other Churches, a renewal of her spirit and vigour, and greater versatility of powers?

England has bestowed on her Hindu subjects, late indeed, and in larger measure and more liberal sense since 1829, all the privileges of her own higher culture and civil order, so far as the people are capable of receiving them; there are now numerous universities and schools of every sort there, widow-burning and exposure of children is forbidden, the administration of justice is organized, the exclusiveness of castes will not be able to hold its ground much longer, countless newspapers and magazines find a large circle of readers. But all this will not suffice to give the millions of India what they chiefly need—a great moral purification and improvement. The inspiring breath of religion can alone effect that. The Christian missions there have accomplished very little in proportion to their efforts and the greatness of their task, and have scarcely stirred the surface of the vast slough of heathenism. Not only in Hindustan; the three hundred years of Catholic and the fifty years of Protestant missions are rich in examples of admirable devotion, persevering energy, and heroic self-sacrifice; noble martyr blood has flowed in streams, and flows still every year. But when we ask for the result of so many sacrifices, and so vast an apparatus, we are disappointed, and can hardly help feeling that the distinguished powers which would have produced such rich fruits at home have been wasted abroad on sterile soil. It is true that many Indian tribes, whose conversion seemed finally achieved, have died out and left no trace, in spite of their Christianity. The once flourishing missions of the Jesuits in North America and Paraguay have long since expired. Even among the cultivated races of India, in Camboja, Siam, and Burmah, only a few

Duty to the Heathen and its Hindrance. 29

thousand converts have been won by the missionary labour of above a thousand years; and, moreover, the Indian Christians have the reputation of getting baptized for interested motives, and easily falling away. It is, above all, one of the rarest things to find a permanent settlement of heathen converts with a native priesthood. As to the Protestant missions, their own friends admit that only a tiny fraction of the heathen population has as yet been, I do not say actually converted, but even prepared for conversion, and that if the apparatus and energies employed are measured by the results, an unfavourable judgment must be formed of the missionary work altogether.

Our surprise is diminished when we discover, on looking into the narratives of missionaries and travellers, how the European Christians carry with them everywhere their divisions and sectarian spirit; how, for instance, in East India, twenty different churches and sects are labouring at the conversion of the Hindus, each endeavouring to encroach upon the rest, destroy their settlements, and gain over their proselytes. And what is true there is true equally elsewhere, so that Christianity presents itself to the intelligent heathen under the repulsive aspect of division and uncertainty.

In Tahiti, the French Government years ago took possession of the Protestant missions and handed them over to French Catholic emissaries. We know how dear this arbitrary procedure cost the Government of Louis Philippe, on account of the pecuniary indemnification paid to the English missionary Pritchard, which was so cried out against in France. In Madagascar, the emissaries of the rival Churches, Catholic and Protestant, brought matters to such a pass that King Radema oscillated for a year between them, and when he was murdered each party charged the other with the crime, and the mutual hatred and endeavours to supplant one another still continue. In 1845 the Protestant missionaries were ejected from Fernando Po by the Spaniards, who laid claim to the island. That is the spectacle presented by Christians to the gaze of the heathen world. Christ says that every kingdom divided against itself shall be destroyed. We understand the failure of missionaries. And that is not all. What is to Christians the holiest and most venerable of all places, the birth-land of our faith, where Christ taught, lived, and suffered, is now the meeting-place of Churches that hate one another. Greeks, Russians, Latins, Armenians, Copts, Jacobites, Protestants of various sects, all have there their fortresses and entrenchments, and are intent on making fresh conquests for the rival Churches. To the shame of the Christian name, Turkish soldiers have to interfere between rival parties of Christians, who would else tear one another to pieces in the holy places, and the Pasha holds the key of the Holy Sepulchre. The strife between Latins and Greeks for the possession of the chapel in 1852 was the immediate occasion of the Crimean war.

Truly every one who values the name of Christian should daily pray to God for a fresh outpouring of the Spirit of Unity, that we may keep a new Pentecost of enlightenment, peace, and brotherly love.

LECTURE III.

DIVISION OF EAST AND WEST: GROUNDS OF HOPE.

WHEN we speak of the hopes of reunion of separated Churches, it is obvious that the first point to be thought of is to prepare the way for a better understanding, for taking counsel together, and for discovering eirenic explanations of the existing confessions of faith. The first thing is to distinguish dogma from opinion, traditional doctrine from the artificial products of theology, use from abuse, to remove well-grounded causes of scandal, and to restore what has become corrupted to its original form. Two divided Churches cannot rush at once into each other's arms, like two friends meeting after a long separation. And we see what infinite difficulty a single difference in doctrine may occasion, and how it may frustrate the most various and well-meant endeavours, in the separation of the Lutheran and Reformed Churches, which is not yet

Division of East and West. 33

by any means wholly got rid of, notwithstanding the grand union between them.[1] There is needed a powerful and dominant spirit of union, such as is not often found in the course of centuries, and a common controlling principle independent of individual caprice. Above all, the union of Churches is only then possible, when a high measure of mental culture is found in connexion with religious intelligence and zeal. From a lower intellectual standpoint differences of rite and ceremonial are regarded as questions on which salvation hinges, and instead of quiet and peaceful inquiry men rush to arms. Among Mahometans almost all differences have been decided by the sword, the restoration of unity meant the conquest and extermination of a sect; and thus religious wars have lasted for centuries among them down to quite recent times. Among Christians religious wars have been chiefly carried on when great moral corruption turned religious zeal into fanaticism, as in the Albigensian wars in the south of France, and the later contests there between Protestants and Catholics.

[1] [The Lutheran and Reformed (or Calvinistic) Churches of Germany were united by Frederick-William III. of Prussia in 1817, under the name of the "Evangelical Church" (*Evangelische Kirche*), which is still the Protestant State Church. But the union was only partially successful. See Krummacher's *Autobiography*, pp. 95, 96.]

If we look round among the nations to see where there is any disposition to take part in the work of pacification, we must put aside the Romance nations, Spanish, Italian, and even French, partly on account of their religious indifference, partly because of their exclusive devotion to political questions and interests; and because too they do not feel the sting of separation, from belonging entirely, or almost entirely, to one Church. Nor can we look to North America, where the sectarian spirit is still in full bloom, and the passion for division is so widely spread. With the Slavonic peoples the national sentiment is just now preponderant, and forces higher religious considerations into the background. There remain England and Germany.

In England the friends of union are a numerous and daily increasing body. The whole movement of the Oxford school, which has been advancing for the last thirty-five years—what used to be called "Puseyism," and is now called "Ritualism"—is essentially, and for the most part consciously, directed to union with the Western Catholic and the Eastern Churches.[1] But, on the other hand, the sharply defined Protestant

[1] For some years past [since 1863] a magazine expressly devoted to this object has been published in England,—the *Union Review*.

spirit and antipathy as well to Rome as to everything, whether in creed or ritual, that exceeds the bare letter of Scripture, is nowhere more deeply rooted in the popular mind than in England. This Calvinistic spirit, as it may well be termed, is peculiarly powerful in the great communities of Baptists, Congregationalists, and Wesleyans, and reacts from them on the members of the Established Church. And there must be a fundamental change in the condition of the Established Church itself, if it means to deal with the question of union in earnest; it must abandon its position as a State Church, which makes it at once too narrow and too broad, too lax and too stiff, too free in one sense and too dependent in another.

And so we come to Germany. In the German Empire the Catholics now form one-third, the Protestants two-thirds of the population. If we count the Austrian provinces, the two Churches are about equal in numbers. This situation is peculiar to us Germans among all nations. Only the two great neighbouring countries of Holland and Switzerland exhibit a somewhat similar phenomenon. In every other nation one Church, whether Roman Catholic, Greek Catholic, or Protestant, immensely preponderates, if it does not prevail alone. But we have suffered so unspeakably from this religious division, which pierces through the body of the nation like a sharp sword, and our weakness, dismemberment, and humiliation, stand in such close relation of cause and effect to our division of Churches, that the belief is constantly forcing itself on every German familiar with the history of his country, that where the religious split began and the schism originated, there the reconciliation must follow, and the division must lead to a higher and better unity. That would be the tragical expiation in the great drama of our history.

Meanwhile the numerical proportion of the members of different Churches is not the main point. Far more important is the relative proportion of powers and capabilities which can neither be counted nor weighed; and this leads to the observation that in Germany the overwhelming preponderance, or rather domination, in science and literature, is on the Protestant side. Our *belles-lettres*, and nearly all our scientific literature, if we except some medical works, is almost entirely Protestant. In theology especially the disproportion is so great that the Protestant theology is at least six times richer than the Catholic in quantity and quality. The main cause of this is unquestionably to be found in the former condition of the Catholic schools and universities; in the oppressive Latin influence, fatal to intellectual life, which lay like a dead weight on the culture and education of Catholic countries, and the defective character of the schools intrusted to a foreign and essentially un-German Order, which through its systematic neglect and contempt of the German language, its inadequate classical teaching and its formal method, failed to implant in its scholars either the capacity or the materials of thought, either style or power of expression, thirst for knowledge, or perseverance in seeking it. For two centuries and a half this state of things continued, and its consequences are still constantly felt. However, for the object we are now considering, the reconciliation of the Churches, this inferiority of one side might tell favourably, and almost be reckoned a gain. For when the end in view is to unite those who are divided, it is essential that at least one party should be conscious of its own deficiencies, and desirous of sharing the benefits and privileges of the other.

The present state of things in Germany is this: Catholics and Protestants are united by community of speech, literature, manners, laws, and administration of justice,

—by everything, in short, which binds men together,—while the gulf between them in Church matters is far wider than that which separates Catholics from members of the Russo-Greek Church. The Protestants have often wished and sought for reunion with the Catholic Church of the West; but there has been only one attempt on their part, almost immediately abandoned, to come to an understanding with the Eastern Church, when, in 1575, the Tübingen theologians entered into negotiations with Jeremiah, Patriarch of Constantinople. But a comparison of their respective confessions then led both parties to the conclusion that the doctrinal and ecclesiastical differences were too great for any union to be effected. Nor could even the transfer of the Protestant Baltic provinces and their university to Russia produce any change in this cool, self-sufficient, and exclusive way of looking at the question. But this cannot continue, and it is certainly indispensable for members of the Latin Catholic Church, as soon as they enter into conciliatory negotiations with Protestants, never to act without reference to the Eastern Church, or, still better, in concert with its members; or else the attempt to bridge over one chasm might help to widen and deepen another no less deplorable and

Division of East and West.

displeasing to God. And to leave out the English Church from our attempts would be to drop a link no less indispensable than precious in the chain we are seeking to reunite.

But we cannot undertake the healing of a schism without first having a clear view of its original causes and subsequent course. Let us begin with the older split. How and why was the Christian East divided from the West?

In the earlier centuries the distinction of Eastern and Western Churches simply meant a distinction in geographical site and language, and hence later on they came often to be called the Greek and Latin Church. As Christianity passed from East to West, all Christian documents and writings were for a long time—till towards the end of the second century—composed in Greek only, and even in Rome the Greek language prevailed for a considerable time among Christians. Thus did the Eastern portion of the Church for a long time enjoy a complete intellectual superiority; the Westerns had to learn from their Greek co-religionists, and to receive from them their ecclesiastical and theological education. All Latin theological literature before St. Augustine is in substance the application or imitation of Greek models. From the fourth century the Bishop of Constantinople advanced more and more to the headship of the whole Eastern Church; and the strength, life, and learning of the Church became more and more concentrated in this imperial metropolis. Rome vainly sought to reduce the dignity of the Bishops and Patriarchs of New Rome, as it was called; it was too completely involved in the circumstances of the Greek Empire, and too well adapted to the needs of the Eastern countries and Churches, and became so indispensable when the other great Sees of Alexandria, Antioch, and Jerusalem had fallen under Moslem dominion, and their Churches were gradually disappearing. After the northern migration each Church went its own way; the union between Rome and Constantinople, often interrupted by quarrels, was always restored after a longer or shorter interval, but the alienation increased. The other Western Churches in Italy, France, England, Spain, and Germany had no direct relations with the East. The establishment of the Carlovingian and afterwards of the German Empire, was regarded at Constantinople as an usurpation and violation of the rights of what claimed to be the sole legitimate representative of the ancient Roman Empire.

Division of East and West.

Moreover, many Roman rites began more and more to vary from the Eastern form, as in the use of unleavened bread in the Eucharist, and afterwards in the withdrawal of the chalice, and disuse of immersion in Baptism. The most important point of difference was the addition of *Filioque* to the common creed, forced by the Franks on Rome after long resistance, whence sprang the controversy about the Procession of the Holy Ghost, which has lasted to this day.

Yet it was not till quite the middle of the twelfth century, notwithstanding all the soreness and growing alienation on both sides, that communion between the Churches was broken off. But the Crusades, the acts of violence perpetrated by the Latins who often behaved insolently to the weaker Greeks, and above all the new system of papal absolutism, to which even the Byzantine Emperors were now expected to succumb, all conspired to make a public and complete breach inevitable. Then, in 1204, a crusading army conquered Constantinople and the greatest part of the Empire, and established a Latin Empire there, which the Popes took under their guidance and protection. The whole Eastern Church was to be Latinized, and a complete system of ecclesiastico-political tyranny was organized—a yoke which seemed utterly intolerable to the Greeks, and produced a deep hatred against the Westerns, especially against Rome, that survived for centuries. The seizure and sacking of the capital followed, with circumstances of horrible atrocity and profanation of churches, and then the split both in feeling and in fact was consummated;—in fact, by Innocent III. arbitrarily imposing Latin Bishops on the Greek Churches, and thereby declaring all Easterns heretics and schismatics. Within sixty years (in 1261) the Latin Empire again fell, and with it fell the violently imposed Latin hierarchy. But the restored Greek Empire was weak and imperilled. The hostility of the West, especially of the Popes, had to be bought off at any price; and so the Emperor let Pope Gregory arrange the terms of union as he pleased at the Council of Lyons in 1274. But to carry it out was impossible in the face of universal opposition, and with the Emperor's death the work fell to pieces. A new union was effected a hundred and sixty years later at Florence, which again was simply a work of necessity and compulsion. The Empire had fallen, with the exception of the capital; all else was in the hands of the Turks, who were preparing to strike the last blow,

Division of East and West.

and it was thought that the Pope alone, through his wealth and authority in the West, could avert it. After long negotiations, in which the Pope and his theologians yielded something, and the Greeks, under compulsion of their Emperor, reluctantly and insincerely submitted to the conditions imposed, the decree of union was drawn up, which has since then continued to be the test required by Rome of all Orientals and Russians coming into her communion. But as the Greeks had only submitted under stress of necessity, the work fell to pieces in the next few years, and two Greek Councils condemned the Florentine decrees.

Already, from the thirteenth century, the conviction had been gaining ground, both in East and West, that the great hindrance to union lay not in theological and ceremonial differences, but in the Roman claims to dominion over Church and State. The Greek Church, relying on its tradition and rich ecclesiastical literature, and clinging tenaciously to all that had been established at the time of the great movements and definitions of the fourth and fifth centuries, was suddenly called upon, in the thirteenth, fifteenth, and sixteenth, to accept a form of absolute monarchical Church-government for which there was no precedent or evidence in its former history and literature, which had been developed in the West first in the ninth and then in the eleventh and twelfth centuries, and there only on the strength of a long series of forgeries and inventions, by which the Western clergy had been deceived. The same means were now of course employed for circumventing the Greeks. In Councils, in conferences, and in writings used against them, they were met with the same forged authorities, or with others constructed for their special benefit; but then the attempt proved generally a failure, for the learned Greeks, of whom there were always a considerable body, were too well informed and too familiar with the views of the ancient Church. The only result of such attempts was an increased mistrust on the side of the Greeks, who got accustomed to reject every overture suspiciously, as an attack on the freedom of the Eastern Church and its loyal adherence to the traditional deposit.

But meanwhile the great and growing Russian Empire had become the centre of Greek Christianity, and the daughter Church of Russia left a mere honorary primacy, without real power, to the mother Church on the Bosphorus and its Patriarch. For 132 years, from 1588 to 1720, Russia had a Patri-

Division of East and West. 45

arch of her own.[1] But in all points of doctrine and usage the Greek type was preserved unchanged. Just at the time of the erection of the Patriarchate began also the efforts of Rome and the Jesuits to bring about an union of the Churches in Poland, which then still included whole districts belonging to the Greek rite, in Lithuania and in Russia. In Poland and Lithuania the attempt succeeded by means of the Bishops taken from noble Polish families. As all the externals of worship were left unchanged, and the question of the *Filioque* was unintelligible both to people and clergy, the union simply consisted in throwing off the Patriarch of Constantinople and submitting to the Pope. All this, however, was the work of force and intrigue, dictated by motives of policy and ambition. The Lithuanians were to be completely separated from the Muscovite Empire, to which they were bound by ties both of race and religion. The antagonism between Russia, which was constantly advancing, and Poland, which was constantly growing weaker and more

[1] [By an ukase of January 25, 1721, Peter the Great abolished the Patriarchate of Moscow, which had been established with the consent of the four Eastern Patriarchs, and substituted the "Most Holy Governing Synod"—the composition of which has been subsequently changed more than once—as the supreme authority in the Russian Church. To this change the Patriarch of Constantinople assented two years afterwards.]

anarchical, has shaped the whole Church-history of the Slavonic world from the middle of the sixteenth century to this day. The attempt of the Poles to seat two impostors (the false Demetriuses) side by side on the Russian throne sprang from the same origin; they were to subjugate the Russian Church to the Pope. The only result attained, after many persecutions and acts of sanguinary violence, was the internal split of the Polish nation. The nobles and higher clergy remained Uniate or Latin, while the people and the lower clergy were Greek, or at least ready and inclined to return to the Russian or separate Greek Church. These unionist efforts conducted by the Jesuits, with their brutal tyranny, have had unforeseen consequences of world-wide import. They have led at once to the aggrandizement of Russia and the downfall of Poland; to the first, by inspiring the Russian people with that crusading spirit or proud national feeling of "the world against us and we against the world," which taught them to regard every foreign war as a war of religion; to the dissolution of Poland, because its religious divisions could not be healed, nor yet be pacified by the establishment of civil equality. Besides the system of elective monarchy and the anarchy and venality of its nobles, the chief cause of the destruction of Poland was religious dissent and the intervention of Russia, when appealed to for the protection of its co-religionists. From the time of Peter the Great Poland was dependent on the will of the Czar, and yet it proceeded with an incomprehensible blindness to exclude its numerous non-Catholic citizens from all offices and posts, and to oppress them in other ways. A long series of religious wars, always carried on with horrible cruelty, extends through the later history of Poland, even over the first partition.

The aggrandizement of Russia since the middle of the seventeenth century had been mainly due to the Czars undertaking the charge of their foreign co-religionists and seeking to draw them over to themselves. Catherine II. wished to reap the harvest sown by her predecessors during the last 130 years, and incorporate Poland, where it was possible, with the Russian Empire. By the two partitions of 1772 and 1793, she had placed whole dioceses of the Uniate Church, including two in Galicia, and in 1796 several millions of Uniates, under Russian rule. From that time forward it became a fixed aim of Russian policy to abolish the union, and to bring back these millions—sometimes by gentle

means, where necessary by violence—into the bosom of
the Greek Church. The higher Polish clergy with the
Jesuits had paved the way for this, by drawing over the
nobility to the Latin rite against the former agreement,
so that the people who had remained true to the Greek
rite felt alienated from them even in religious matters.
The clergy themselves had often Latinized, and thereby
increased the confusion and division. And so it was
easy for the Russian government to dissolve the union
in this kingdom divided against itself. The method
adopted was to leave the people to choose whether to
remain Latins or to return to the " Mother Church."
They almost always chose the latter. Under the Czar
Nicholas, up to 1839, there were two million Uniates
in Russia, but by an ukase of March 25 that year,
they also were brought over to the national Church.
And so at last of the great Uniate Church of the north,
which once contained several millions, there is nothing
left but a few poor fragments in the diocese of Ohelm.
And Catherine understood well enough to whom she
owed her chief successes in Poland ; when Clement XIV.
suppressed the Jesuit Order,[1] she received them grate-

[1] [The Jesuit Order was suppressed by Clement XIV. (Ganganelli) in 1773, and restored by Pius VII. in 1814, when some of its older members were still alive.]

Division of East and West.

fully as educators of the Polish nobility and counsellors of the Kings and Bishops who had played so effectively into the hands of Russia. By her command the Order with its revenues continued to exist in her dominions.

The long history of this union, this ecclesiastical tragedy, which had its beginning, middle, and end in violence, persecution, oppression, and bloodshed, and closed with the destruction of a once mighty kingdom, teaches us how a union of divided Churches is not to be effected.

In Galicia, South Hungary, and Transylvania, there are still Uniate Churches, including together two millions and a half of souls. But everywhere the mixture of the Roman and Greek rite, or the superseding of the latter by the former, which a section of the clergy are always aiming at, causes disturbances and perplexity of conscience, and endangers the continuance of the union.

In general, the Eastern Church has remained where it was when the two halves of Christendom were still in communion. Since then it has been disturbed by no important doctrinal controversies, and there has accordingly been no occasion for dogmatic definitions. Its theology has remained thoroughly patristic and traditional, keeping to the writings of the Fathers up to the seventh century, and practically closing with St. John of Damascus in the eighth, while the theological movement of the West began in the ninth, culminated with the scholasticism of the thirteenth and fourteenth centuries, and then again in the sixteenth and seventeenth had to encounter its great adversary, the Protestant doctrine and theology. Even in the twelfth century, although there were many points in dispute between Rome and Constantinople, it was still the prevalent view that there was but one great universal Church, embracing East and West alike. The national hatred was great, but neither side dared to say this, "We alone are the Catholic Church, and you are excommunicated, apostate, heretical." Both sides appealed to the first seven or eight Œcumenical Councils and their decrees, and held that fresh decisions binding the universal Church could only be enacted at such another Synod representing both East and West. And that is still the belief in the East and in Russia. With this is connected the patriarchal theory, that there are five Presidents of the whole Church, four in the East and one in the West, namely, the Pope, to whom belongs the first rank, but no power or dominion over the rest. But

Division of East and West.

since the Pope has separated himself from the communion of the rest, and put forward inadmissible claims to dominion, his place has been taken by the later Patriarchate of Moscow, and since 1720 by the Governing Synod of St. Petersburg which superseded it; and if any controversy concerning the whole Church required settlement, it would be referred to the four Oriental patriarchs, and decided by their unanimous verdict.

Thus it was that before 1854 the doctrinal differences between East and West were very slight, but the differences in Church constitution, ritual, and worship were considerable.

The insertion of the *Filioque* in the Nicene Creed is an offence to the Orientals, who say that the Latin Church alone had no right to make it, and that this ancient symbol must be maintained in the precise form fixed by the Œcumenical Councils. The Popes allowed it to remain without the addition in the (Uniate) Eastern Churches. So again with Purgatory. All Oriental Churches rejected the notion of a purifying fire after death, and at the Council of Florence the Pope and his theologians consented to its being abandoned or left an open question, and the doctrine of the Church confined to the permission or recommendation of prayer for the dead.¹ No objection was ever made to the use of the chalice in the East, though the Popes persistently refused it to Western nations, or withdrew it after being once conceded, at the cost of rivers of blood and of the strengthening and extension of Protestantism. So again with the marriage of priests. The universal custom of Russia and the East, that every secular priest should marry before ordination, was never assailed by the Popes, nor did they ever require the introduction of celibacy. It was out of regard for the Greek Church that at the Council of Trent no condemnation was pronounced on divorce for adultery, as an error, and the Council contented itself with vindicating the opposite practice of the Latin Church.²

As regards Baptism, which the Orientals perform by

[1] [This is all that is taught authoritatively now. The Council of Trent (Sess. xxv.) simply defines " Purgatorium esse, animasque ibi detentas fidelium suffragiis, potissimum vero acceptabili altaris sacrificio juvari," and forbids preachers to deal with subtle and difficult questions, which tend rather to curiosity and superstition than to edification. Perrone, the Jesuit Professor at the Roman College for the last thirty years, says accordingly, " Duo tantum ab Ecclesiâ de Purgatorio definita sunt, ejusdem scilicet existentia, et suffragiorum utilitas erga defunctorum animas. Omnia proinde quæ ad locum, tempus, pœnarum naturam et acerbitatem spectant, dogma non attingunt ; prout nec attingunt quæ ad modum pertinent, quo defunctorum animæ suffragiis fidelium adjuvantur."—*Prælect. Theol.* Parisiis, 1854, vol. i. pp. 478, 9. The Greek Synod of Bethlehem, held in 1672, on this, as on other points, virtually indorsed the teaching of Trent.]

[2] [Divorce *a vinculo* is not however allowed among the Uniates.]

Division of East and West.

immersion, while throughout the West, both Catholic and Protestant, affusion only is used, in Constantinople it was for some time the custom to reject Western baptism and rebaptize converts. In Russia, also, a Synod held in 1620, under the Patriarch Philaret, prescribed this rebaptism, but the Philaret of our own day observes that it was an order not to be justified by the doctrine of the Church, but excusable on account of the crimes of the age.[1] Latterly Constantinople has followed the advice of St. Petersburg, and abandoned the practice of rebaptizing, thereby admitting the validity of Western baptism.

Even the official language of Rome used to speak not of heresy but only of schism, which had come to be termed the Photian Schism—an unhistorical designation, for Photius, who came forward in the ninth century as the accuser of Rome and the West, did not effect any separation, and the mutual recognition and intercommunion of the Churches lasted two centuries longer. Indeed, as late as 1583, Pope Gregory XIII. addressed a friendly letter to Jeremiah, Patriarch of Constantinople, calling him his "venerable brother," and breathing no syllable about subjection or recanta-

[1] Philaret's *Geschichte Russlands*, trans. by Blumenthal, 1872, vol. ii. p. 98.

tion of any doctrine, but only begging him to exert his authority for the reception of the new calendar in the East.[1] And the ecclesiastical acts of the separated Eastern Bishops and Priests have been acknowledged as valid in the West on the ground of their episcopal succession and ordination, as was distinctly shown at the Council of Florence, where neither the Pope nor his theologians maintained that they had lost their jurisdiction (or power of absolution) through separation from Rome.

The great stumblingblock and real hindrance to any understanding in the eyes of all Easterns is the Papacy, in the form which it has assumed according to the ultramontane theory, since the time of Gregory VII., of an absolute spiritual and temporal dominion over the whole Christian world. Both Latins and Greeks said as much in the middle ages, and it is still openly avowed in our own day, as well by converts as by Russians and Greeks themselves.[2] And now, through recent occurrences, every hope of reconciliation and future reunion has been purposely cut up by the roots. The present Pope has within the last few years imposed

[1] See Theiner's *Die Staatskirche Russlands*, 1853, p. 47.

[2] Cf. *e.g.* Prince Augustine Galizin's *L'Eglise Græco-Russe*, Paris, 1861, p. 59.

Division of East and West. 55

three new articles of faith—the Immaculate Conception, his Universal Episcopate, and his Infallibility. None of his predecessors for 1800 years, with one solitary exception, has done anything of the kind, and that one, Boniface VIII., contented himself with a single dogma, and did not succeed in securing the acceptance of that.[1] The whole traditions of the Eastern Church, its canon law and patristic literature, contain nothing in support of these doctrines, or capable of being brought into harmony with them. The forgeries employed to persuade the Greeks to accept them have long since been seen through and exposed.

In Rome the mind and temper of the Greeks and Russians was perfectly well understood. It was known that on their principles this attempt to make new dogmas could only be regarded as a crime and a blasphemy. The division can no longer, as before, be called a mere separation or schism; the whole Eastern and Russian Church, with its seventy-five millions, must now be declared heretical, and the Curia and

[1] [The author refers to the Bull *Unam Sanctam*, issued in 1302, defining that the spiritual and temporal swords are equally committed by God to the Roman Pontiff, and that it is absolutely essential to salvation for every human being to be subject to him. The Bull was publicly burnt at Paris, and Philip the Fair appealed to a future General Council. It was virtually withdrawn by Clement V.]

Jesuits must admit all the consequences that follow from that declaration. To speak any longer of hopes of a future union would border on madness. We can but assume that this was deliberately intended at Rome —entire separation for ever and for all eternity. But man proposes and God disposes.

The Russian people—viz., the thinking and active portion of them, who form public opinion—believe that two great tasks lie before them, one in Europe, the other in Asia. The latter is the strengthening and maintenance of Christianity, everywhere in Asia oppressed by Islam, and the restoration of a great Asiatic Eastern Church. The Privy Councillor Mouravieff, a member of the Governing Synod, refers to this point when he says:—"We are thoroughly convinced that the famous Oriental Sees will recover their ancient splendour."[1] Indeed, the system of the Russian and the whole Eastern Church requires that the three ancient Patriarchs of Alexandria, Antioch, and Jerusalem, should again become in fact what they were formerly, and not be mere assessors of the Patriarch of Constantinople. In Europe it is the idea of Panslavism which shapes the thought of young

[1] *Question Religieuse d'Orient et d'Occident,* p. 97.

Division of East and West.

Russia, the ruling and acting Russia of the future. And not there only, but throughout Eastern Europe, this notion or hope is strongly leavening the popular mind, into which it sinks deeper every day. Yet the object aimed at, whether it be the moral or political union of all Slavonic peoples, or of the ten principal cognate races, which comprise together some eighty millions, has no historical basis, and has never before found expression or sympathy. For the first time, in our own day, some Bohemian scholars, who had advanced from linguistic to historical investigations, discovered that all these nationalities united by a common primitive language sprung from a common stock. It was a natural inference from this in Russia, that the Russian nation itself, comprising fifty-four millions of the eighty million Slaves, was called to the hegemony of the race. When the question is regarded from an ecclesiastical point of view, we find that over two-thirds, or fifty-six millions, of the Slaves belong to the Greek Church, nineteen millions to the Roman Catholic, three millions to the Uniate, and about a million and a half are Protestants. And thus the Panslavist idea naturally points to the formation of a great united Slavonic Church, in which seventy-eight million Slaves might be religiously welded together through a union of Latins and Easterns. Even now, a letter of the Czech historian and leader, Palacky, to the Russian spokesman of Panslavism, Pogodin, is going the round of the daily papers.[1] Palacky salutes him as "the reawakener and apostle of the happy idea of Slavonic national union," and adds, "Praise and thanks to the all-merciful God, who has blessed your labours and mine. The Slavonic national spirit has waked up from the slumber of centuries; the sentiment of common fellowship is constantly gaining ground in all Slavonic countries. The ultimate triumph of the cause we, who are both old, may leave with confidence to the rising generation." That younger generation will soon discover, if it has not discovered already, that, with the mass of the people, no community of mind and sentiment, such as is aimed at, is possible without an union of Churches. The Czechs may consult the Russians about that.

Since the time of Alexander II. a powerful movement has penetrated the Russian Church. It feels itself to be the chief representative and leader of the Eastern Church, so venerable for its age, its unbroken

[1] See *Wiener Neue Freie Presse*, 10 Feb. 1872.

Division of East and West.

succession, and its immutability. Even the independent Church of the kingdom of Greece is stirring, and in the South and Russian North alike an ecclesiastical literature is rapidly growing up. Foreign, and especially German literature, is read and studied. Several young men in Greece have received their theological training at German universities. And at the same time energetic efforts are being made in the Russian Church to secure the reforms which are urgently needed. It is perceived that the whole position of the clergy, the feud between the white and black clergy—the seculars and parish priests on one side, and the monks and bishops, who are taken from their ranks, on the other —and the want of preaching and popular instruction, are matters requiring radical change. This is not only felt but openly asserted; and those who remember the days of the Emperor Nicholas cannot but be astonished at the advances made since then. And this Church is able to correct any past mistake or error, as has been done in the case of rebaptism, even should it affect the decree of a Council. She is not compelled by her principles, on the ground of any fancied infallibility, always to drag her errors after her like a ball fastened to her heel. And accordingly there is ground for the fairest hopes in that quarter of the Christian world.

LECTURE IV.

THE GERMAN REFORMATION.

THERE are not many years in the world's history where two eventful pages come so close together as on March 16 and November 1, 1517. On the former day the fifth Lateran Council at Rome was closed after several years' session, and thereby the last hope of any reform of the Church from above was laid in the grave. That assembly of Italian bishops had but one object, to extend the power of the Pope, and make any independent reforming Council, like the Council of Basle, impossible for the future.[1] Seven months later Luther's theses were posted up at Wittemberg, and the contest began which, after 350 years, is still unfinished.

[1] [The fifth Lateran Synod was opened by Julius II. in 1512, and dissolved in 1517 by Leo X. It consisted of some fifty or sixty Italian bishops only, and has never been received as œcumenical, nor did even ultramontane writers, till quite lately, venture to affirm its œcumenicity with any confidence; Bellarmine and Muzzarelli, *e.g.* speak very doubtfully. Its principal achievements were the abolition of the Pragmatic Sanction, and the assertion, in the Bull *Pastor Æternus*, of the superiority of Popes to Councils, in direct contradiction to the famous decrees of Constance.]

The German Reformation.

The Reformation was a movement so deeply rooted in the needs of the age, and sprang so inevitably from the ecclesiastical conditions of the centuries immediately preceding, that it took possession of all the nations of the West in turn. So powerfully did it sway men's minds in Italy, the native home of the Papacy, that Paul IV. declared the Inquisition, with its dungeons and blazing pyres, to be the only sure and firm support of the Papacy there. In Italy and Spain, however, it was found possible to crush the movement, though only at a frightful sacrifice of human life; but in Germany it sank so deep into the heart of the nation that even such a tribunal as the Spanish Inquisition would have failed to achieve the task.

This force and strength of the Reformation was only in part due to the personality of the man who was its author and spokesman in Germany. It was Luther's overpowering greatness and wonderful many-sidedness of mind that made him the man of his age and his people. Nor was there ever a German who had such an intuitive knowledge of his countrymen, and was again so completely possessed, not to say absorbed, by the national sentiment, as the Augustinian monk of Wittemberg. The mind and spirit of the Germans was in his hand what the lyre is in the hand of a skilled musician. He had given them more than any man in Christian days ever gave his people—language, popular manuals of instruction, Bibles, hymnology. All his opponents could offer in place of it, and all the reply they could make to him, was insipid, colourless, and feeble, by the side of his transporting eloquence. They stammered; he spoke. He alone has impressed the indelible stamp of his mind on the German language and the German intellect, and even those among us who hold him in religious detestation, as the great heresiarch and seducer of the nation, are constrained, in spite of themselves, to speak with his words and think with his thoughts.

And yet still more powerful than this Titan of the world of mind was the yearning of the German people for deliverance from the bonds of a corrupted Church system. Had no Luther arisen Germany would not have remained Catholic. We may gather that from the enthusiastic sympathy, especially in South Germany, for the doctrine of the Anabaptists. This doctrine, which emanated from the lowest ranks, was zealously attacked by the whole body of theologians. It was essentially distinguished from Luther's teaching, whose favourite dogma of justification by faith alone it re-

The German Reformation.

jected. But many laid down their lives for this form of belief, and if the princes had not hastily combined to strangle the movement, which was not only religious, but political and social, in the blood of its adherents, Germany would probably have been divided, not, as afterwards happened, between Lutherans and Zwinglians, but between Anabaptists and Lutherans. For the Reformed (Zwinglian) doctrine was never popular in Germany; it was a mere exotic growth, artificially fostered by the princes, and was generally only endured under compulsion.

Luther had one very powerful ally besides the national sympathy, and that was the Court of Rome itself. Had the Curia been advised by an astute disciple of the German Reformer, he could hardly have given counsel more efficient or more profitable to his master than what was actually followed. At the first moment, the official theologian of the Curia, Sylvester Prierio, Master of the Sacred Palace, met Luther's appeal to the Bible with the assertion that the force and authority of Holy Scripture is derived entirely from the Pope. To censure anything done by Rome was heresy. Then, again, Leo X.'s Bull against Luther condemned as errors such universally familiar truths as that the best penance is reformation of life, and that it is against the charity of the Holy Ghost to burn heretics. If the indulgence-preachers told men that as soon as the money chinks in the chest the soul flies out of Purgatory, they preached to deaf ears.

But if Luther and the other Reformers painted in the darkest colours the deep corruption in the Church, the wretched management of ecclesiastical affairs, the crimes of the clergy, and the unspeakable misery of the people, so utterly neglected, deceived, and plundered by their pastors, all this was fully admitted on the other side. And more than this too: the Popes themselves could not deny—for it was too notorious—that Rome itself was the seat and source of corruption, and the Popes its authors and disseminators. Adrian VI. had it openly proclaimed at the Diet of Nuremberg in 1522, that everything in the Church had been perverted, and a disease had spread from the head to the members, from the Popes to the rest of the rulers of the Church.[1] And what Adrian proclaimed in general, in accents of penitence, the Germans read in detail twelve years later in the

[1] [Adrian VI., a Netherlander, who succeeded Leo X. in 1522, was a man of deep piety, but he reigned only one year. He was the last non-Italian Pope.]

The German Reformation. 65

famous memorial drawn up at the command of Paul III. by nine Roman prelates, including Caraffa, afterwards Paul IV., where the theory invented by sycophants of the Pope's absolute dominion over the whole Church was characterized as the source of all this corruption.[1] One member of the Commission, Cardinal Contarini, who was afterwards papal legate in Germany, expressly maintained the impiety of this doctrine, which made the Pope absolute lord and master of the whole Church, and defended Luther's work on the Babylonish Captivity, where the doctrine of Christian liberty is opposed to this tyrannical doctrine.

What was communicated to the Emperor Charles V. as the wish and advice of the Pope, was mainly comprised in the request to put down the German movement by force of arms. The Legate Campeggio represented in 1530 that capital punishment and the establishment of the Inquisition in all German countries

[1] [Paul III. commenced his reign by summoning several distinguished men of reforming tendencies and devout life into the Sacred College, among whom were Contarini, Pole, Sadolet, Caraffa, and Giberto; and they were encouraged to speak their opinions freely. See Ranke's *Popes*, vol. i. pp. 98 *sqq*. It was, however, through Caraffa's influence, who distrusted all gentler means of gaining over the Protestants, aided by the advice of Ignatius Loyola, that the Roman Inquisition was established in 1542, and he became one of the first and severest Grand Inquisitors. *Ib.* pp. 141 *sqq.*]

would be the best remedy.¹ And when at last the Emperor took up arms, Paul III. sent an auxiliary force commanded by his nephews. And thus the feeling of hatred against Rome was so universal, that Marcellus II., when legate in Germany, wrote to Rome that nothing so filled him with fear and horror as the intense exasperation of a whole nation, which he everywhere encountered.² Even a Jesuit living in Rome, John Faure, in 1750 felt obliged to acknowledge that the principal and indeed only cause of the separation of the Northern nations was, not at all their love for Lutheran and Calvinist doctrines, but their hatred of the Pope and Court of Rome, and this hatred was increased by the profligacy, pride, domineering, and covetousness of the clergy, especially of the religious orders.³

This too was remarkable and hard to explain, that after the famous Bull issued by Leo X. in 1520 against the earliest publications of Luther, the Popes refrained from any further dogmatic pronouncements. Europe was in a state of the extremest excitement, and the

---

¹ So thought Clement VII. according to Cardinal Loaysa. See *Cartas al Emperador Carlos V. por su Confesor.* Heine, Berlin, 1848.

² Cf. *Anecdota Romana.*

³ *Commentarium in Bullam Pauli III.*, 1750, p. 139.

whole religious edifice seemed tottering to its fall. The most discordant doctrines, in sharp antagonism to all previous teaching, were forcing their way to the front; never had there been a period in all Christian history when the perplexity of men's minds was so great, and the people left to themselves so utterly helpless, as in the forty-three years from 1520 to 1563. Yet the Popes, according to the latest theory the sole infallible teachers of mankind, kept silence. Not a single doctrinal Bull of that whole period exists; one whole generation was suffered to grow up in Europe, and another to pass to its grave, without knowing what the infallible chair in Rome bade them believe on the gravest religious questions. German Bishops, like Faber in Vienna, made the most moving representations. The whole generation, he said, whose birth or youth coincided with the time of the great controversy, knew not what was the true religion, and if this continued men would become thoroughly godless and atheistical.[1] As late as 1530 he wrote to the Pope that, if even then he would undertake the correction of abuses, there was great hope that all Germany, and indeed the whole Church, would be brought back to its earlier condition of

[1] Raynaldus, *Annal. Eccl.* ann. 1536, p. 70.

peaceful orthodoxy.[1] But all was in vain. The Popes persisted in their policy of silence, and of putting every obstacle in the way of the Council so anxiously looked for, until it was too late for its decrees to make the slightest impression on a generation that had been thoroughly imbued with Protestant views from childhood.

And the German Church? Where was it then, and how did it help itself? The Germans had still indeed a political unity—the Empire, with the Emperor and the Imperial Diet; and they had Bishops and dioceses. But there was wanting a higher organization of common life, —in a word, a German national Church. For centuries no German Council had been held, nor anything done to remedy even the grossest and most crying abuses. In truth, such a Council was hardly possible, and it is a significant fact that during the whole forty years of the Reformation contest, neither the German episcopate, nor even any considerable portion of it, made a single attempt to take counsel in Synod on the religious situation and the common measures to be adopted. There is scarcely a parallel case in all Church history, but it is explained by their conscious impotence. For since the dismemberment of the entire Church system through

[1] Raynald. *Annal. Eccl.* ann. 1536, p. 54.

The German Reformation. 69

the Popes, the German Church lay on the ground like a helpless and motionless giant with fettered limbs.

The whole conduct of the Popes from Clement VII. downwards, in regard to the constantly renewed petitions and requirements of the Emperor, the sovereigns, and the nations, as recent discoveries have revealed it to us, was one long series of evasions, intrigues, and falsehoods. Pius IV. himself declared without hesitation to the Venetian ambassador, that his predecessors had professed to wish for a Council, but had not really desired it. And he added, that if he wished after their example to give the mere appearance of a Council, he could keep the world occupied for three or four years at least with the question of when it should meet.[1] Many may find it incomprehensible how, at a time when one nation after another was being swept into the movement, the authorities at Rome should have obstinately persisted in refusing what they must have themselves acknowledged to be just and right; but three causes conspired to produce this result. The first was the powerful and compact resistance of the whole *entourage* of a Pope and his court, which profited by the abuses. The second cause lay in the diminution of

[1] Cf. Reimarus, *Forschungen zur deutschen Geschichte,* pp. 594, 602.

power which any reform must inevitably involve. For the development of the papal system, with its centralized bureaucracy and plenary power to meddle in everything, had sunk the Church in such deep degradation that every removal of an abuse, every improvement in doctrine and discipline, would have been also a lessening or limitation of papal power. Lastly and chiefly, it was the supreme principle and soul of the whole Roman system of ecclesiastical administration that made the Papacy hostile to all reform—the principle, namely, that a claim once preferred could never be abandoned, an error or injustice never publicly confessed, and therefore never remedied. Authority must remain inviolate, and can never be sufficiently exalted. This was pre-eminently the principle of the new Order of Jesuits, which now came to the assistance of the Papacy in its sore need. And this soon appeared in the great question of the use of the chalice, which the sovereigns, who in other respects were entirely opposed to Protestantism, were now urging, because they saw no other way of retaining their subjects in the ancient Church. But the Jesuits, Canisius especially, carried the day by insisting that the point at issue was the authority of the Church, meaning that of the Pope, for

The German Reformation. 71

which alone they cared. If any concession was made, how was the earlier conduct of the Popes to be excused, with the bloody wars and countless holocausts of human victims it had cost?[1]

When we look closely into the circumstances of Germany during the period from 1520 to 1568, we perceive how the resistance of the old Catholic element became constantly feebler and the number of Catholics more limited, till at last the Protestant belief, like a mighty stream, swept everything before it. In a former work I have taken pains to discover all the German scholars who still adhered to the ancient Church, or would gladly have remained loyal to it, but it was a mere handful. In the reports of papal nuncios during thirty years we read that there were still many so-called "Expectants," who wished to remain undecided till a true Council pointed out to them the right way. We read how these nuncios were adjured and implored with tears by the highest personages, by princes, to impress on the conscience of the Pope the urgent necessity of at once convoking an Œcumenical or a German Council as the only available means of saving the Church. But, generally speaking, all the learning and culture

[1] Cf. *Canisii Vita*, p. 199.

gravitated to the Protestant side, especially the influential class of schoolmasters and humanists, and even the clergy. These last were still very numerous at the beginning of the movement, for the German Church was the wealthiest in the world. The endowed benefices were numberless; even small towns had from thirty to forty priests, besides convents and monks, and we see these clergy going over in shoals to the Reformation, or succumbing without the slightest resistance to the introduction of Protestantism. In those countries and cities where the new religion had been imposed by the civil authority or the magistrates, the Catholic clergy did not depart, as they easily might have done, but stayed where they were, partly in voluntary partly in involuntary subjection. Even the dissolution of the monasteries only converted the monks into Protestant preachers, or followers of some secular calling. And yet in South Germany there were hundreds of unoccupied parishes and empty monasteries, where the priests and monks ejected by the Reformation would have been gladly welcomed and cared for, had they come. And this too at a time when all over Europe, in France, England, the Netherlands, Italy, Spain, fagots were blazing, and men preferred a fiery death to denying their faith.

The German Reformation.

In 1557 the Venetian ambassador, Badoero, who was well informed, reported that seven-tenths of the German nation had become Lutheran, and two-tenths belonged to other sects—the Reformed and Anabaptist, —while only one-tenth remained Catholic. The greater part of Austria and Bohemia was Protestant, and in Bavaria, the nobility, and the Emperor Maximilian II. himself, though he continued nominally Catholic, were of the same religion. But since the end of the sixteenth and beginning of the seventeenth century, half Germany has gradually become Catholic again. This happened partly through the internal division of the Protestants and the litigious spirit of their divines, which produced disgust and painful uncertainty among the people, and led many to look on the rigid system of authority and uniformity of the ancient Church as preferable. But it was chiefly by the oppression and banishment of the Protestant ministers, the forced emigration of those who adhered to their faith, the destruction of Protestant Bibles, catechisms, and hymn-books, and generally the employment of all those means of coercion which the Jesuits had reduced to a system, that the so-called counter-Reformation in Austria and Bavaria and the ecclesiastical principalities was brought about.

But the notion of a permanent separation from the ancient Church had not occurred to the generation of the Reformation era in Germany. It was only a reformation that was demanded; it had been longed for and demanded for centuries before. The old dwelling-house was thought to require repairing and cleansing, but there was no intention of pulling it down and building a new one in its place. The idea of two rival Churches in Germany arrayed in permanent hostility against each other shocked the mind. All diets and religious conferences of the day were conducted on the assumption that the adherents of the new and the old religion were still members of one universal Church, and that a common understanding could and ought to be arrived at, and communion of worship restored. Even when the Augsburg religious treaty of 1555 established a legal and political separation, the Estates of the Empire consoled themselves and the nation with the hope of a future Council; and as that could not be at once obtained, they thought another religious conference should be tried, when, as was said, " the truth would be brought to light." Two years later this conference was opened without any result at Worms. But still for a long time the separation continued to be regarded as a

The German Reformation. 75

temporary and provisional state of things, although it seemed as if the Tridentine decrees on the one side, and the Formulary of Concord[1] on the other, in their sharp antithesis must exclude all hope. Yet a century after the separation the hope of a future union was still clung to in the Articles of the Westphalian Peace, and the boundary-lines were fixed *only until*, " by the grace of God," a friendly settlement of the religious controversies was attained.[2]

With the year 1560, at the end of the reign of the Emperor Ferdinand I., a revolution began to work in Germany, and generally both in the Catholic and the Protestant camp, which could not fail to make even any approach to friendly negotiations more difficult, and seemed destined to make the breach perpetual. Among the German Protestants the long series of internal controversies was decided in a strictly Lutheran sense, and the building up of the Lutheran dogmatic system followed,—a theological codification studiously sharpening all the points of divergence from the ancient Church. It was based on the Formulary of Concord, which was not a common symbol like

[1] [The *Formula Concordiæ* was established in 1577, after Luther's death, as the final and formal standard of Lutheran doctrine.]

[2] Cf. *Instrum. Pacis Westphal.* v. 14, 25, 31, 48.

the Augsburg Confession, but a theological code which the princes enforced by all the means of compulsion at their command. Thenceforward all attempts at peace and re-union necessarily ceased. Still more fatal was the change which took place in the Catholic Church, coinciding with the latter period of the Council of Trent and the rise of the Jesuit Order. Hitherto, since 1540, and partly before, there had been a considerable body of learned men in the Church, who were attached indeed to the Catholic doctrine and communion, but at the same time recommended radical reforms and a return to the earlier and purer system of the Church, and were accordingly in favour of making great concessions to the Protestant party. Such had been, in Germany, Erasmus and his friends, and then Witzel, Staphylus, Cassander, Wild (or Ferus), and, in France, d'Espense, Gentien, Hervet, the Chancellor l'Hôpital, and others. The gentle Emperor Ferdinand I. was substantially of the same mind, differing therein from his brother Charles V., who took the Spanish view, and only saw in all the movements of the age a heresy to be rooted out with fire and sword. Ferdinand and his son Maximilian II. still hoped for a reconciliation. Ferdinand procured the drawing up of

The German Reformation.

the eirenical memorials of Cassander and Witzel, and for a long time demanded more searching reforms from the Council of Trent. He did not obtain them, and at last agreed, though reluctantly, to the Council being closed without having satisfied even the most moderate requirements of Church reform.

The writings of Witzel and Cassander on one side, and the opinions and influence of the contemporary Jesuits, Laynez, Salmeron, and Canisius, on the other, reveal the wide chasm which was on the point of opening within the Catholic Church. The former started from the principle that, to use Cassander's words addressed to the Emperor Ferdinand, the view and judgment of the ancient Church must be investigated, in order that, as far as possible, the present Church, which was descended from it, might be restored to the form it assumed in its free development after Constantine, at the period of the first Councils. Cassander adds that the authority of this ancient Church is so fully recognised, that both sides, even those who are wont to appeal to Scripture only, appeal to its verdict. The Jesuits devoted themselves to enforcing the opposite view. According to their representation the Church is a great all-embracing Empire, an absolute monarchy, ruled with irresponsible and plenary power by one man, the Pope. To him all alike, layman and cleric, king and beggar, are equally and absolutely subject. No one has any rights before him, and all authority in the Church is an emanation from his—a mere deputed power that may at any moment be recalled. This papal kingdom must be upheld and extended by all means of compulsion and violence, and punishments of life and limb, sometimes directly inflicted, sometimes by invoking the secular arm, which is bound at once to execute its sentence. To make any sort of concession to the rebellious and disobedient would be simply to put a premium on rebellion. Moreover, the Papacy requires large revenues and constant influx of money from the whole world, partly on account of the enormous expenses involved in the administration of a kingdom of 200 millions descending into the minutest details, partly that it may be able to reward liberally its numerous ministers and instruments. And therefore all reforms calculated in any way to diminish the papal income are for that reason, if for no other, inadmissible.

There could not, of course, but be bitter enmity between the reforming school of Catholic theologians and the Jesuits, and Witzel said with good reason, "We are the object of their fiercest enmity, because they wish to preserve the present deformed condition of the Church, and, according to the principles of their Order, will allow no improvement."[1] The leading men of this party soon died off, and those who inherited their ideas had to keep silence and conceal themselves, for the Jesuits in a rapid course of victory gained possession of the Catholic high schools and gymnasia, and became confessors and directors of conscience at the Courts, and who then would have dared in Catholic Germany to disown their rule or breathe a single notion displeasing to them? Moreover, every work which suggested any concessions at all being made to the adherents of the Reformation was promptly condemned at Rome, and every such opinion compromised the author's safety. And thus on both such sides any approximation seemed impossible. In all the domains of Catholic princes Protestant worship was suppressed, under Jesuit dictation; it was the professed aim of the Order to undermine the treaty of Augsburg. Everything was rapidly tending to the Thirty Years' War.

[1] See his letters to Cassander in 1565, shortly before his death, in *Illusrium et Clarorum Virorum Epistolæ*, Batav. 1617, p. 280.

Here I must refer to a peculiar difficulty which stands in the way of any approximation or friendly understanding between the German Protestant Church and one of the ancient Churches. I mean the interruption of ecclesiastical succession, the abolition of the episcopate and episcopal ordination of Presbyters. There was no external necessity for Luther and his colleagues to do this, for some of the Catholic bishops had early come over to their side. But they thought that, as in the New Testament the words *bishop* and *presbyter* are used interchangeably, and the two offices were not at first distinguished, the episcopate must be regarded as a mere later and human institution. But with it much more too was lost, more than at first sight they themselves comprehended; the link which attached them to the old apostolic Church was severed, and the bridge broken down by means of which communion or mutual exercise of influence between the two bodies might have been maintained or reopened. This appeared also in their relation to the English Church, which had equally issued from the Reformation, but had retained the episcopate, and with it the succession and ordination. Consequently, any German Protestant minister who wished to enter its service had first to

The German Reformation.

undergo episcopal ordination, whereas a Latin or Greek priest coming over to its communion is received at once by virtue of his former orders, the validity of which is acknowledged. And on episcopal ordination depends the consecration of the Holy Eucharist and absolution. And all this was sacrificed on the strength of a doubtful interpretation of Scripture, for not a few Protestant theologians held that the episcopate was instituted by the Apostles, though in the later apostolic age; and all must allow that the whole history of the Church from the death of the Apostles exhibits a settled episcopate existing everywhere, and indeed is completely shaped by it.

Two distinguished philosophers, Leibnitz and the Court preacher Jablonski, about 1701, when Prussia became a kingdom, perceived the gravity of the false position into which the German Reformed Church had brought herself, and busied themselves with considering how the defect might be remedied. Leibnitz thought it would have been better if the Reformers had not broken the "linea ordinationis" (the succession) legitimately preserved in ancient Christendom, and the bishops had retained their former position, and priests been ordained by bishops, as before.[1] Jablonski took a similar view. He thought the episcopate had been abolished in order to outrage the Roman Church as much as possible, whereby also all the Eastern Churches, the English, and all Christian antiquity, was set at nought. And he added that its restoration was the more to be wished, because it almost seemed as though in separating from the Roman Church they had separated from the universal Church also; but he did not deny that there were great difficulties in the way of such a restoration, which could only be overcome "by a large measure of heroic spirit."[2]

Both representations were addressed to the King of Prussia, and Frederick I. actually, on assuming the royal title, had two preachers, Ursinus and Sander, consecrated bishops by the English Church, but with their death this episcopate again became extinct. In our own days Frederick-William IV. again took up the subject, and this was one of his reasons for urging the establishment of a Protestant bishopric at Jerusalem. Here a bishop of the English Church was to impart ordination to German clergymen; and in the

[1] See Joh. Esth. Kapfen's *Einige Vertrauten Briefe*, Leipzig, 1745, p. 250.   [2] Cf. *Henke's Magazin*, 1795. No. 222.

King's instructions occur the words, which have evidently been carefully chosen, that "he offers his hand with full confidence to the episcopal Church of England, which unites with evangelical principles an historical constitution and ecclesiastical independence aiming at universality." This is a gentle but perfectly intelligible expression of the feeling that his own Church was too much isolated and alienated from the great ancient communions; and it is in fact well known that he was dissatisfied with his "sovereign episcopate," and would gladly have intrusted the guidance of the Church to fitter hands, meaning thereby an episcopal constitution.

LECTURE V.

REACTION TOWARDS UNION ON THE CONTINENT IN THE SEVENTEENTH CENTURY.

THE Germans displayed a quite remarkable patience in attempting for nearly a century to heal the religious schism by means of public conferences, the latest of which took place in 1601 at Ratisbon, and 1618 at Prague. But this only resulted in scholastic disputations, in which everything turned on dialectical skill and promptness, and the one point aimed at was to perplex the adversary and involve him in a contradiction. The upshot, as a rule, was simply to widen the chasm, and increase mutual bitterness, without any real gain to either side. And that always will be the result when each party starts with the conviction of its own absolute perfection, and seeks nothing but victory and the conversion of opponents to its own views.

In the period succeeding the Thirty Years' War, many

Reaction of Seventeenth Century. 85

members of the Lutheran Church felt uncomfortable and dissatisfied with their position. There was something oppressive and humiliating in the yoke of civil domination over the Church, and its entire dependence on secular princes and their theological advisers. It is true that the scandalous and violent changes of the religion of whole countries, such as took place in the Palatinate, in Anhalt, and elsewhere, ceased after the Westphalian Peace, and the religious changes of sovereigns affected themselves only. But still the whole Church system remained in the hands of Consistories, under royal control. And to this must be added the theological ossification and narrow rigidity of the doctrines which had to be maintained according to the Formulary of Concord. From these causes sprang a double reaction, among the laity and the theologians. The lay reaction manifested itself partly in the growing frequency of conversions to Catholicism; many felt the authority of Popes and Councils to be preferable to that of a secular prince. On the other hand, the whole religious literature of the laity, from the seventeenth to far into the eighteenth century, is penetrated with a profound dissatisfaction at the condition of the system and prevalent teaching of the

Protestant Church. The theological reaction was chiefly developed in the writings and school of George Calixtus, as represented at the two universities of Helmstadt and Königsberg. Calixtus insisted on the authority of ecclesiastical tradition, rightly understood, viz., the consentient teaching of the first five centuries, being recognised as well as the scriptural evidence of doctrine. And thus he approximated to the ancient Churches, both Eastern and Latin, and evoked the most vigorous opposition. His view, which is now shared by so many of the very best men, that the three particular Churches should not regard themselves as faultless and incapable of improvement, found no acceptance then on either side.

Meanwhile, towards the end of the seventeenth century the number of converts to the Catholic Church increased. Queen Christina, the talented and accomplished daughter of Gustavus Adolphus, resigned the Swedish throne to embrace Catholicism, in order to take refuge in the ship of ecclesiastical authority from the ocean of philosophical doubt. Still more remarkable was the conversion of the learned Landgrave of Hesse-Rhineland, who, after twenty years' experience, wrote a book full of well-meant but unsparing exposure of the abuses he had discovered in the Church of his choice. The motives of several other conversions of princes and princesses about the same period were less disinterested.

Further influences co-operated to produce in thinking Protestants a longing, if not for the Catholic Church, for the appropriation of its prerogatives. The Netherlander, Hugo Grotius, who was celebrated throughout Europe as an acute and many-sided scholar, had in his widely circulated writings insisted far more strongly than Calixtus on the profound and excessive divergence of Protestantism from the Church of the early centuries, and the necessity of either seeking a reunion with the ancient Church, or at least restoring much which had been rejected. And afterwards a great impression was produced by the accession of a truly pious and model Pope in the person of Innocent XI. (1676-1689), who was at once engaged in earnest conflict with the Jesuits, and made an attempt, feeble and ineffectual as it proved, to put a check on their pernicious system of morals. He was the only Pope who made such advances to the Protestants as entirely to approve the negotiations of Spinola, which were based on extensive concessions. But his participation had to be kept secret, and Spinola was obliged to act in his own name, without appealing to the plenary powers granted him by the Pope, because the French Cardinals in Rome were opposed to the scheme.[1] A religious reconciliation with Germany would then, as afterwards, have been very inconvenient for French policy.

These labours for reunion commenced in Germany in 1675, and lasted about thirty years. Royas de Spinola, a Spaniard who had come to Germany as confessor of the Emperor Leopold's wife, and was made bishop first of Teria (in Croatia), and then of Neustadt near Vienna, was the first to undertake the enterprise. Germany was still suffering from the effects of the Thirty Years' War, and the Jesuits, who were its authors, were as powerful as ever at the Courts of Paris and Vienna. Both the Emperor Leopold and Louis XIV. had intrusted their consciences to them, and followed their counsel implicitly in religious matters; and if the houses of Hapsburg and Bourbon were united, and abandoned their feud of 150 years' standing, they seemed strong enough to crush Protestantism on the Continent, the more so as it had no powerful protector

[1] [Some account of Spinola's labours, and of the negotiations for union in the seventeenth century generally, may be found in two articles on "Leibnitz's Letters on Reunion," in the *Contemporary Review* for May and August 1867.]

to fall back upon. But there was no prospect of this, owing to the hostile attitude assumed by Louis towards the imperial house and the German Empire. The Emperor Leopold was so deeply interested in the success of the undertaking that he at last brought the negotiations for union to Vienna, and summoned Leibnitz thither.

On the German Protestant side stood Leibnitz and Molanus, the latter a well-grounded theologian of the school of Calixtus; the former the leading mind of Germany at that date, equally acute and capacious, and of immense knowledge—an universal genius in his day, like Aristotle of old, and in fact the first who raised the credit of Germany before the world after the deep decay of the seventeenth century. After a while, Bossuet, the most influential of the French bishops, who might almost be called the theological oracle of his age, was brought into the negotiations through the intervention of some royal ladies.[1] Bossuet's famous *Exposition of the Catholic Faith* had appeared some time before, and had at once been translated into all languages. The aim of his book was to distinguish

[1] [Especially of Anna Gonzaga of Mantua, wife of Edward, Count Palatine.]

what is really dogma from theological opinions and inferences, and to place it before Protestants in the least repellent form. It had been approved and commended in Rome by Pope and Cardinals, and has almost attained and preserved down to our own day the authority of a Confession of Faith. Now, of course, like so many other writings and views, it is abolished and become obsolete, for it says nothing of the new articles of faith fabricated since 1854, and characterizes as mere school opinions what are now proposed as Divine revelations. Thus Bossuet puts aside the question of Infallibility, as a mere scholastic controversy having no relation to faith; and this was approved at Rome at the time. Now, of course, he is no longer regarded in his own country as the classical theologian and most eminent doctor of modern times, but as a man who devoted his most learned and comprehensive work, the labour of many years, to the establishment and defence of a fundamental error, and spent many years of his life in the perversion of facts and distortion of authorities. For that must be the present verdict of every infallibilist on Bossuet.

At that time the first condition in all such negotiations, which had to be demanded on the Catholic side, was that the Protestants should no longer regard and designate the Pope as Antichrist, and when this was agreed upon Spinola and Molanus thought a great point was gained. For this view was still universally prevalent, and dominated the thoughts and feelings of the people to such a degree that a contemporary theologian, Hermann of Hurdt, could write to his colleague Fabricius of Helmstadt that "all Protestants are so bewitched with this conceit about Antichrist, that they fly from Catholics as from snakes in the garden, and think they see a dragon or an evil spirit if they meet a Catholic."[1] According to the received view, the apocalyptic images of the harlot seated on the beast, who is drunk with the blood of the saints and disciples of Jesus, and of Babylon that deceived the nations, were not to be understood of heathen but of papal Rome, and the Pope himself as the Antichrist of Scripture,—a view put forward by the Protestant divines as the foundation of their religion, though it is inconsistent with Scripture and involves fatal contradictions. But Rome was partly responsible for its growth. If the Pope was constantly urging on religious wars, and recommending the extermination of all

[1] *Mensel's Magazin*, 1788, p. 118.

heretics by the sword—and even at Rome executions for Protestantism continued down into the seventeenth century,—the people were sure to think they saw the Papacy in the apocalyptic woman drunk with the blood of the saints, just as it was easy to identify the Man of Sin spoken of by St. Paul, who exalts himself above everything divine, and sits in the temple of God, with the Pope, claiming to be vicar of God, and to exercise absolute dominion over all nations and Churches. Untenable as these interpretations are critically, they have had an enormous influence. At the time of the Reformation many thought this the only ground which would justify them in conscience in separating from the old Church and establishing a new one. For it is said of Babylon or Rome in the Apocalypse, "Come out of her, My people, that ye be not partakers in her sins." Even during the last century these views have had an enormous influence, and have built up a brazen wall between Catholics and Protestants. At this hour they are still deeply rooted and powerful in England and America, and supported by a copious and constantly increasing apocalyptic literature. But in Germany they have long since disappeared from the popular belief, notwithstanding the sanction of the Smalkaldic

Articles, and thereby, as it seems to me, one of the most serious hindrances to a reunion of the two religions is removed.[1]

But at the end of the seventeenth century it was very different in Germany. Then the song was sung year by year in every Evangelical congregation—

> "Defend us by thy word, O Lord,
> From Pope and Paynim's murderous sword,"[2]

and the events of almost every year supplied a practical commentary on this juxtaposition of the two great enemies. In Hungary there had been a bloody persecution of Protestants, lasting ten years, and it was notorious to all the world how Louis XIV. treated the Reformed in France. The preachers therefore were never at a loss for opportunities of asking the prayers of their congregations for co-religionists suffering under Antichristian tyranny. And the feeling thus engendered made it impossible to bring theological negotiations for reunion before the public; on the contrary, such attempts had to be kept strictly private.

[1] [See first Appendix in the author's *First Age of Christianity and the Church* (W. H. Allen and Co.), on "History of Interpretation of 2 Thess. ii. 12."]

[2] [Cf. the popular Scotch ditty quoted in Scott's *Abbot*—
> "The Paip, that Pagan fu' o' pride,
> Hath blinded us ower lang."]

Leibnitz did not become a Catholic privately, as has been inferred from his unpublished work discovered in MS. some fifty years ago, the so-called *Systema Theologicum*. This work was only meant to show what a thinking man might urge from the Catholic standpoint in favour of the controverted Catholic dogmas. He did not indeed adhere to the Protestant form of belief, in which there was much that he disapproved. He wrote to the Landgrave of Hesse that had he been born in the Catholic Church he should never have left it, but that he could not join it while certain doctrines continued to be enforced in all their naked harshness. He thought the Protestants ought to accept any doctrine proved to have been universally received in the ancient Church of the Roman Empire. And in fact Molanus had already managed to get rid of so many difficulties that Bossuet thought the union would be pretty well accomplished if the other theologians assented to his view. But both Leibnitz and Molanus considered it essential that the Tridentine Council, with its manifold anathemas, should be suspended, and the controverted points examined and compared at a new Council, composed of Catholics and Protestants in common. Leibnitz appealed in support of this view to the concessions made at Basle to the Hussites. A still better example would have been the Council of Florence, where all the points of difference with the Greeks were allowed to be re-examined and compared by both sides together, without regard to the decrees of the Council of Lyons in 1274.[1] This condition however proved fatal to the whole scheme.

The greatest difficulties, the stumblingblocks which could not be removed, did not even come under discussion, or were only incidentally referred to. That same Molanus, who showed himself so conciliatory and almost Catholic in matters of doctrine, afterwards maintained against his colleagues that the revocation of the edict of Nantes, and the persecution of Protestants in France, with the formal approval of these proceedings by the very best of the Popes, Innocent XI., had done more to confirm him in drawing a line between Protestant and Papal doctrine than all the controversial divinity he had ever seen.[2] Yet even Bossuet

[1] [The Council of Florence was accordingly to have been accepted on both sides, had the reunion proved permanent, as the *Eighth* Œcumenical Council, passing over all the mediæval Councils since the separation of East and West. It is actually called *Octavum Concilium* in the first Latin issue of the Acts, published in 1526 under Clement VII., and thirty years later in Cardinal Pole's *Reformatio Angliæ*, a collection of statutes made by him in his legatine capacity, and published at Rome in 1566.]

[2] See the letter in Leukfeld's *Antiquitates Amelunstbornenses,* p. 113.

was unable to see, what must have been so clear to every thinking man, that a Church which makes a rule and principle of coercing conscience and exterminating heretics by the sword, can only inspire hatred and detestation. There was one Pope, however, Clement XIV., who does appear to have seen it. He says, "What a happy revolution would have been witnessed, if, instead of being persecuted, heretics had simply been entreated and adjured with all possible gentleness not to separate from the centre of unity; if their difficulties had been explained with kindness, their objections patiently listened to, and if, above all, they had been addressed, as religion itself speaks, without bitterness or pride."[1] I don't know whether Ganganelli remembered, when he wrote this, that he was condemning a long line of his predecessors, and above all the canonized Pius V.

There were other hostile and menacing circumstances in the background of these negotiations for union, which cast a dark shadow over every gleam of hope. Chief among these was the Roman notion of the absolute power of the Pope, and all attempts in apologetic writings and expositions, such as Bossuet's and Veron's

[1] *Lettere Interessanti di Clemente XIV.*, Ninezia, 1778, iv. 60.

before him, to explain this away, or make it look harmless and beneficial, were sure in the end to prove illusory. No Protestant ever judged the Papacy more favourably than Leibnitz, who wished to see the temporal power of the Popes still further increased and extended over the whole of Italy, that they might be the better able to act as European arbiters, and hinder wars of conquest. But an unlimited despotic power, such as the Jesuits and all the Romanist party ascribed to the Court of Rome, he considered equally intolerable and mischievous. Then again it was a standing reproach and objection urged against every representation of Catholic doctrine put out for the benefit of Protestants, that what looked good and innocent on paper had in fact, and in its practical application to popular life, a very different and most objectionable character. This feeling was vividly expressed in the universal contradiction to Bossuet's representation evoked in Protestant Europe. Even Molanus did not conceal his conviction that the Papal Church was far worse in worship than in doctrine, as he had witnessed it in Italy, Spain, and other Catholic countries; it was, indeed, so corrupted that a thinking man, unacquainted with the Reformed doctrine, could not but suppose the Christian religion was a political invention of the Popes for keeping men in subjection.[1] The utter helplessness of the disputants in this matter was brought to light when they came to consider, in view of a future union, how the worst excrescences of a crude and immoral superstition, by the help of which the religious Orders preyed upon the people, could be restrained. But with the independent position of these Orders, and their financial wants, nobody had any effective remedy to suggest. Leibnitz says in one place,—" The great question is still this— how far it is allowable to wink at the public corruptions, especially when it looks as if the steps taken amounted to a tacit approval of them."[2]

Bossuet's biographer, Cardinal Bausset, cannot explain by what fatality these promising efforts after union, after proceeding so far, and with so rich a combination of talent, learning, and good-will engaged in the cause, came to nothing, and left no trace behind them. He thinks the interposition of Leibnitz frightened the theologians, and ruined everything. Far from it; on the contrary, Leibnitz would have made concessions which the theologians shrank from. The real reason

[1] *Höck, Anton Ulrich,* p. 113.
[2] See *Rheinfeld Briefwechsel,* ed. Bömmel, ii. 78.

was a different one. In dealing with a Church where the actual creed of daily life differs so widely from the theoretical creed, it is impossible to get beyond mere theoretical negotiations. Bossuet himself did not choose to see that; whenever any gross abuse was brought before him, he would always point triumphantly to the substance of the doctrine, which contained nothing of the kind. And yet the great bishop and famous doctor might himself have been pointed out as a conspicuous example of ecclesiastical impotence. He found himself, in his own Church, in presence of a doctrine invented only a century before, which could not but have a most decisive influence on the religious position of every Christian,—the doctrine that fear alone, without love of God, is sufficient for the remission of sins. He considered this a most dangerous error, affecting the very essence of Christianity, and wrote against it; but he could not prevent the most powerful of the religious Orders, with the knowledge and support of the Holy See, taking this error under its patronage, and acting upon it in the confessional in his own diocese. Yet he found it quite in order that every one who had desired to administer Communion according to Christ's institution, simply for the sake of union and obedience, should have been excommunicated. For theologians understand well how to strain out gnats and swallow camels.

After these fruitless attempts of Bossuet, Molanus, and Leibnitz, nothing further of the kind was undertaken for 170 years, either in Germany or elsewhere.[1] Men were thoroughly discouraged and deterred. On the Protestant side, the gradual advance of rationalism hindered any further thought of union, and among Catholics there could be no idea of reviving those efforts till after the abolition of the Jesuits in 1773. But they had too much to do in setting their own house in order, and the best of them thought they could only invite the guests they wished to see when the house had been cleansed. In our own day there are phenomena which exhibit a real or apparent affinity with the ideas and efforts it is the aim of these Lectures to suggest to the minds of believing Christians. Many would reckon among these the "Evangelical Alliance," a British and American product of a kind of unionist sentiment. But this association, of which very little has been heard lately, has confined itself to a mere external

[1] [The correspondence of Archbishop Wake with the doctors of the Sorbonne early in the eighteenth century had a similar aim, though it led to no result.]

combination and common action of all Protestant communities for an offensive and defensive alliance against the ancient Churches. The fusion of the Lutheran and Reformed Churches brought about by Frederick-William III. has remained a mere fragmentary work, and has led to internal divisions, the end of which is yet to be seen; and one of the most eminent Protestant theologians, Kahnis, has declared only this year that "the introduction of the union into the Lutheran national Churches of Germany, Russia, and Scandinavia, would be the beginning of incurable discords which would probably end in their dissolution. To carry it out generally is an impossibility."[1] The fundamental principle of this union, which is to leave the most opposite doctrines to co-exist side by side, unmodified and unreconciled, and let every one choose between them, has not succeeded.

The recently formed community of the Irvingites might be regarded as in some sense a favourable symptom, pointing to hopes of union. It includes some highly respectable men, familiar with ecclesiastical antiquity. The exclusive product of a Protestant soil, and founded by men trained in Protestant belief, it approxi-

[1] *Christenthum und Lutherthum*, Leipsic, 1872.

mates in essential points to the ancient Churches of East and West. It reminds one strongly of a phenomenon of the second century, Montanism. Perhaps it is still possible to strip off from the system much which appears to those who look at it from without too fantastical and directly contradictory to the mind of the ancient Church, such as the revival of the Apostolate, and the immediate expectation of the great crisis of the world's history intimated in Scripture.

Where faith and love are found, there hope cannot be absent. He who believes in Christ, and loves his country and Christians of all confessions, cannot divest himself of the hope that no distant future may reveal a Church which, as the genuine heir and representative of the Church of the early centuries, may have room and power of attraction for those who are now separated; a Church where liberty will be reconciled with order, discipline, morality, and unity of faith with science and freedom of inquiry.

LECTURE VI.

THE ENGLISH REFORMATION, ITS NATURE AND RESULTS.

AT the beginning of the Reformation the island kingdom of England was far behind-hand in power, wealth, and population; indeed, 150 years later it had only five million inhabitants. It possessed no fleets, no manufactures, no colonies, and no army. But it was better prepared ecclesiastically than the Latin countries for receiving the seed brought over from Germany. From the end of the thirteenth century, and constantly during the fourteenth, it had resisted the encroachments and extortionate demands of the Roman Court with the united force of King and Parliament. And Wycliffe, one of Luther's forerunners, and the Lollard sect, had disseminated doctrines which partly corresponded with those proclaimed at Wittenberg. But it was from above, and not from beneath, as in Germany, from the Crown, not from the people, that the ecclesiastical revolution in England received its impulse, rule, and form. No man of first-rate eminence appeared—no Luther, or Calvin, or Melanchthon—to take the lead of the movement. Minds of an inferior order, possessed with the ideas struck out at Wittenberg and Zurich, served as the instruments for naturalizing those principles in England and effecting the ecclesiastical changes.

It is well known that what brought about the breach with Rome and the transference of the papal supremacy to the King was the affair of Henry VIII.'s divorce. The whole English clergy submitted, renounced the Pope, and promised to regard him henceforth only as Bishop of Rome. One bishop alone, Fisher of Rochester, resisted, and went to the scaffold. There was no intention, however, of separating from communion with the Pope; and his rights in relation to the universal Church, such as the summoning and presiding over General Councils, were not called in question. The people were expressly assured that England continued to be a portion of the Catholic Church, of which the Roman Church was another branch.[1] Nor was there any change of doctrine introduced. But a series of Acts

[1] In the *Institution of a Christian Man*, 1537, approved by twenty-one Bishops. See *Formularies of Faith* (Oxford, 1825), p. 55.

The English Reformation. 105

were passed—the Parliament being entirely at one with the King—which extended the royal authority over the Church further, until at last all ecclesiastical power seemed to be derived from the Crown. The notion invented by the sycophants of Rome since the thirteenth century, that the episcopal was a mere derivation from the papal authority, was now in England transferred to the Crown.

Clement VII. had already excommunicated the King, but in 1538 appeared a Bull of his successor, Paul III., which excited universal astonishment, for it almost looked as if he wished to alienate the whole nation from him, and drive it into complete separation from the See of Rome. He not only deposed the King and consigned him to eternal perdition, if he did not appear before his tribunal, but laid all England under an interdict, which means, according to Roman teaching, that a Pope punishes and imperils the salvation of millions of innocent persons for the sins of one or a few guilty persons. He forbade all divine worship and administration of sacraments,[1] forbade every Englishman to obey any royal command, deprived all

[1] [There are some exceptions to this rule. Baptism can be administered to children, and the last sacraments to the dying, under an interdict, and confessions can be heard.—Cf. Soglia, *Instit. Jur. Priv. Eccl.*, Paris, p. 556.]

the King's adherents of their civil rights, abrogated all treaties made with them or oaths sworn to them, prohibited all traffic with them, and gave up the property of all Englishmen to be plundered by foreigners. And this was done in 1538, when a great part of Germany and Switzerland, and the northern kingdoms, had already risen against Rome, and thousands in Europe were eager to make capital out of such weak points of the Roman See, and thus increase the widely-spread abhorrence of the Curia. It might really be regarded as an example of judicial blindness.

After Henry's death in 1547 the Reformation was carried further in a Protestant sense under Edward VI., always from above, by means of the royal supremacy over the Church. Archbishop Cranmer, and Somerset, who was regent for his nephew, a boy of ten years old, worked together, not without opposition from the mass of the people, who were still Catholic in their sympathies; and there were revolts, which had to be extinguished in blood. For the nobility seized the Church property, the country people took up arms, the class of small landowners disappeared, and tenant-farmers took their place. But among the clergy there was only passive submission.

The whole edifice of the new religion collapsed when Mary, the daughter of a Spanish mother and wife of Philip II. of Spain, succeeded to the throne on the early death of Edward. Unreservedly devoted to the Pope, full of burning hatred against the new heresy, and hard and pitiless as her father, she at once broke the promise given to the people, when they rose in her favour, of leaving the laws of the land unaltered. She surrounded herself with like-minded counsellors, and a Parliament elected under strong government influence seconded all her plans. Cardinal Pole appeared, as papal legate, to absolve the nation from the anathemas of Rome, and England found itself again under the dominion of the Pope. The nation was soon taught at how dear a price of human life it had again become Roman. Hitherto the Protestant doctrine had made little advance in the minds of the people, the majority of whom adhered to their ancestral faith ; the decided Protestants could be named and counted. But now the papal legate, Cardinal Pole, the man who ruled England both in religious and civil matters, was himself charged with suspicion of heresy by the terrible Paul IV.—the Pope who saw no salvation for Italy or the world except in the dungeons and piles of the Inquisition,—and was summoned to Rome to answer for his faith. He did not go, but left his implacable persecution and extermination of heretics to bear witness before the Pope and the Roman Inquisition to his unimpeachable orthodoxy. And thus within three years about 300 persons were burnt, including some bishops, several priests, and fifty-five women.

Hundreds of thousands of Protestant writings scattered over the length and breadth of the land, and disseminated in the cottages of the poor, would not have done so much to strengthen the Protestant doctrine as the spectacle of the fires of Smithfield, and the testimony borne by so many men and women, most of whom could have purchased their lives by recantation, going with such wonderful courage to the stake. The impression then made has remained to this day powerfully and indelibly impressed on the popular mind. And if the hatred of everything called Popery has shown itself for the last three centuries stronger and deeper in England than in any other nation, Mary and her counsellors are responsible for the origin of a feeling which was no doubt afterwards intensified by the Gunpowder Plot.

Mary carried with her to the grave the hatred and

detestation of her people; and her sister Elizabeth mounted the throne in 1558 amid loud and universal rejoicings. The re-establishment of papal domination had not obtained much favour even among the populace, whose sympathies were Catholic, and Paul IV. himself took care that the new Queen should have no choice. He made it a question of life and death for her to abjure Rome. When she announced her accession to him, he replied by censuring her "presumption," and declaring that she had been stigmatized by his predecessors as illegitimate, and therefore incapable of succeeding, and that the decision on the subject belonged to him alone as suzerain of England, a pretension of Rome long since rejected by Parliament.

The supremacy over the Church which her father and brother had enjoyed was now again assigned by Parliament to the Queen, who thereby took the place of the Pope. The Act of Uniformity imposed on all Churches the use of the Liturgy of Edward VI., modified in a Catholic sense.[1] Every clergyman was required, on pain of deprivation, to take the Oath of Royal

[1] [That is, the Second Liturgy of Edward VI. It had been the Queen's original wish and intention to restore the First, and with some Catholic additions; but it was found necessary to abandon the design, in order to conciliate the extreme, or, as it was afterwards called, Puritan party.—See Hook's *Life of Archbishop Parker*, pp. 158 *sqq.*]

Supremacy, and out of 9000 only about 189, or one in fifty, refused it.[1] Most of the bishops refused, and new ones were appointed and validly ordained, so that the succession was not interrupted. A short formulary of faith, in Thirty-nine Articles, setting forth substantially the Protestant doctrine, but in modified form and with many compromises, became law. And thus the Reformation in England and the edifice of the English episcopal Church was completed. It differed from all reformed Churches of the Continent, but wished to remain in connexion with them; and the political situation forced Elizabeth more and more into the position of a protector of European Protestantism generally.

Meanwhile the number of Catholics was still considerable, but as all churches and chapels belonged to the dominant religion, and absence from service was punished with fines, they took part in public worship; and thus to all outward appearance there seemed to be but one Church in the country, and every likelihood of the old faith dying out in one or two generations. This state of things lasted till about 1570, when new priests,

[1] [This must be taken with some reserve. The Supremacy Oath was certainly imposed by law from the first; but there is reason to believe that for many years of Elizabeth's reign the majority of the clergy abstained from taking it, with the tacit connivance of the Government. There is no evidence of more than about 800 being sworn in 1559.]

The English Reformation.

trained in the strictest Roman system, came to England from the clerical seminaries established on the Continent, and the Jesuits also commenced their labours there. Then, for the first time, many separated themselves from the national worship; and then, too, appeared the Bull of Pius V., which not only deposed Elizabeth, but forbade all Englishmen to acknowledge her on pain of excommunication, without, however, proposing any other king or regent for their allegiance. And thus all Catholics who did not rebel were excommunicated, and it seemed to be the sole aim of the Pope, who had already tried to get Elizabeth put out of the way by assassination, to produce a general confusion and bloody civil war in England.

The most zealous of the Papal party wanted to make Philip of Spain master of England. A series of plots, conspiracies, and revolts followed. Elizabeth could say with truth that her life was daily threatened, and more than any other in Europe. A new Bull of Sixtus V., issued in 1588 in support of the Spanish invasion, renewed her deposition, on the express ground that the Pope alone was entitled to decide who should wear the English crown.[1] Well might Urban VIII. say after-

[1] [It is remarkable, however, that Sixtus V., one of the ablest Popes of

wards that the Popes, his predecessors, were responsible for the loss of England.[1] The laws against foreign priests were now made more stringent, and the mere performance of sacerdotal functions became a capital offence. A considerable number of priests were actually executed, who showed great constancy in death. The first who were condemned were questioned as to whether they would obey the Pope or the laws of the land in civil matters, and those who answered in the latter sense were spared.

Meanwhile the Jesuits had developed their doctrine of tyrannicide into a system, and had disseminated it both by writing and orally. They taught that, as the Pope has a divine right, in the interest of religion, to depose monarchs and annul all their official acts, the deposed monarch, if he tries to retain his dignity, is an usurper and tyrant, and may be put to death. That this teaching endangered the life of every prince dis-

the post-Reformation era, personally entertained a strong sympathy for Elizabeth, and to the last cherished hopes of her conversion. At one time he even requested Henry III. of France to enter into communication with her on the subject, and he seems to have given only a reluctant sanction to the Spanish Armada. On the other hand, Elizabeth, when urged by her ministers to marry, was wont to reply, "I know of but one man worthy of my hand, and that is Sixtus V."—Cf. Hübner's *Life and Times of Sixtus V.*, passim.]

[1] [A similar remark is attributed to Pius IV. in reference to Paul IV.'s policy.]

The English Reformation. 113

pleasing to the Court of Rome was shown in the murder of Henry III. of France, and the attempts on the life of Henry IV., and of William of Orange, for these two princes also at last fell beneath the daggers of fanatics. And if there was already a disposition in England to look on every Catholic as a born enemy of the State and its rulers, this was further increased by the Gunpowder Plot at the beginning of James I.'s reign, which filled up the measure of the misfortunes of the unhappy adherents of the old Church. The discovery of this Satanic plot for blowing up King and Parliament was commemorated in England by a Church festival, only recently abolished. Pope Clement VIII., who had some years previously urged Henry IV. to assist the King of Spain in conquering England, had just before directed the Catholics to hinder the accession of James, and English Jesuits were deeply implicated in the plot, of whom two were found guilty and executed, and one escaped. King James, with the view of providing some protection for his own life and that of his son, introduced, in concurrence with Parliament, a special oath for Catholics—the Oath of Allegiance. They were to abjure, as impious and heretical, the doctrine that the

Pope can depose sovereigns and absolve subjects from their oath of allegiance, and that princes excommunicated by the Pope may be deposed and murdered. The sorely oppressed Catholics, whose condition had been rendered much worse by the last conspiracy, were to gain some toleration by taking this oath; but Paul v. forbade their taking it on pain of damnation, and all Catholics who took it were to be refused the sacraments. And Cardinal Bellarmine wrote a treatise to prove its unlawfulness.

Meanwhile no express declaration of the Roman Court, explaining in what the soul-destroying character of the oath consisted, could be obtained by any entreaties, and many priests suffered death rather than take it. James, who, from various political grounds, and partly from fear, wished to be on peaceable terms with the See of Rome, intimated to the Pope, through the French ambassador, that he would acknowledge him as the first bishop and president of the Church, if he would renounce the arrogant claim to depose sovereigns. But Paul replied that he could not do so without falling into heresy himself. This conduct of the Pope's made the condition of Catholics in England a terribly painful one—the priests threatened with death

The English Reformation.

on the scaffold, and the laity objects of universal suspicion, detested by their fellow-countrymen and subjected to heavy exactions. There seemed no prospect left them but of constant diminution and gradual extinction; and in fact they had dwindled down to 150,000 by 1630, according to the report of the Papal nuncio, Panzani. Well might they represent to Rome, through Father Leander, that they had suffered more for the Papacy than any other Catholics.[1] Father Leander also represented that Charles I. was surprised to find that doctrines allowed in France were condemned in England. It was universally said that the

[1] [Father Leander, an English Benedictine, was sent to England by Urban VIII. in 1632, and Father Panzani, an Oratorian of Arezzo, in 1634, both with the sanction of the Government, as well to examine and report on the condition of the English Roman Catholics as on the true state of the Church of England. On the latter point they reported very favourably, and the idea of a reunion was seriously entertained on both sides, though it eventually fell through, chiefly owing to the bitter opposition of the Jesuits on one side, and the Puritans on the other. Father Leander reports of the Anglicans: "They agree in all the doctrine of the Trinity and Incarnation and true Deity of our Blessed Saviour; in the points of Providence, predestination, justification, necessity of good works, co-operation of free will with the grace of God. · They admit the first four General Councils, the three authentic symbols of the Apostles, Nice or Constantinople, and of St. Athanasius, as they are received in the Roman Church: they reverence the primitive Church and unanimous consent of the ancient Fathers, and all traditions and ceremonies which can be sufficiently proved by testimony of antiquity: they admit a settled liturgy taken out of the Roman liturgy, distinction of orders, bishops, priests, and deacons, in distinct habits from the laity, and divers other points in which no transmarine Protestants do agree."—*Clarendon State Papers*, vol. i. p. 207; quoted also in Charles Butler's *Book of the Roman Catholic*

Popes vindicated the doctrines whereby the authors of the Gunpowder Plot excused their murderous attack on the King and the nobility.

But now, as before, it was all in vain. The Popes had again and again been told that the notion of murder committed in the interests of religion being meritorious, was so widely spread, so disgraceful and injurious to Catholicism, and so strongly confirmed by Jesuit writings, that there was urgent need for one Pope at least publicly and solemnly to condemn this error. But Rome held her peace; it was impossible even to get the worst of the Jesuit writings which recommended tyrannicide placed on the Index.

The events which occurred in Ireland served to intensify the hatred of the English nation against Rome and the Catholics, and to exhibit the Popes as the most irreconcilable and dangerous enemies of England. On

Church, p. 2. And he adds: "Union seemeth possible enough, if the points were discussed in an assembly of moderate men, without contention or desire of victory, but out of a sincere desire of Christian union ; especially since the learneder sort of Protestants hold this difference to be no impediment to salvation, and grant besides that the Church of Rome is a true member of the Church of Christ."—*Ibid.* p. 208. On the other hand, Montague, Bishop of Chichester, assured Panzani that only three out of the whole bench of Bishops could be considered opposed to the scheme.—*Panzani's Memoirs*, p. 246. It is clear from Heylin's *Life of Laud* that the primate was favourably disposed towards it. See for further information on these negotiations an interesting essay on "1636 and 1866," in *Essays on Reunion*, Hayes, 1867, and cf. *infra*, p. 121.]

The English Reformation. 117

the pretext that the Emperor Constantine had given all islands to the Pope, Adrian IV. had bestowed Ireland on Henry II., king of England. At the time of the Wars of the Roses the English rule over Ireland had again collapsed. The Popes had impressed on the Irish that their island was a papal fief over which they exercised supreme rights of suzerainty, and accordingly, when the English kings ceased to discharge the duties of vassals, Gregory XIII. had sent an English theologian, Sanders, as his legate to Ireland, with Italian officers, and appointed an Irish general, Desmond, to rouse the inhabitants, who had been deprived of the exercise of Catholic worship without having become Protestants, and to lead them in a holy war against England. The enterprise failed, and at the death of Elizabeth in 1603 Ireland was completely subjected to England.

Then broke out the insurrection of 1642, and a massacre followed in which several thousand Protestants were killed. A papal nuncio, Runiccini, came, and for some time acquired possession of supreme power. Ireland was to be entirely separated from England, and annexed either to Spain or to some Italian principality under the suzerainty of the Pope.[1] Cromwell's con-

[1] Ranke, *Eng. Gesch.*, *Werke*, vol. xvii. p. 26.

quest of Ireland put an end to this scheme. At the Restoration in 1660, a prospect was held out to the Irish Catholics of religious toleration and regaining their property, on condition of their taking an oath of allegiance to the King, and repudiating all right of the Pope to depose him or absolve his subjects from the duty of civil obedience. A similar declaration had been required of the English Catholics in 1647 by Parliament, on the motion of Lord Fairfax, as the condition of religious toleration. But Innocent X. had at once strictly forbidden them to accept any declaration of the kind, and excommunicated those who had already subscribed it. And now almost the whole property of Catholics and the social existence of the nobility was at stake in Ireland. But the papal nuncio at Brussels, and the Irish Bishops who were under him, condemned in accordance with papal teaching the "Remonstrance," which 121 nobles had already signed. The theologians who drew it up, Walsh, Carew, and Coppinger, were persecuted and censured, and thus the fate of Ireland was sealed for centuries. This result was most gratifying to the Cromwellian soldiers and English and Scotch adventurers, who had come into possession of the property through the war and confiscations.

The English Reformation. 119

King Charles confirmed them in their possessions, and also confirmed the suppression of Catholic worship. The Catholic nobility of Ireland fell, the entire property passed into Protestant hands, and the mass of the Catholic population sank into an ignorant and barbarous proletariate. But the Pope's right to depose kings, annul oaths, and command rebellion, was preserved inviolate!

Elizabeth and her advisers had attempted to weld together in the edifice of their State Church foreign and mutually hostile elements, which were now sure to conflict with each other. The notion of two or more different Churches dwelling peacefully side by side was at that time hardly thought conceivable, and only admitted as a last resource, under pressure of extreme necessity. And therefore the national Church had to be made capacious enough to embrace and tolerate in its bosom the two opposite parties already existing in England,—the Calvinist and the Catholic.

Calvinism, chiefly represented by the exiles who had returned from Switzerland after Mary's death, and forced their way into Church offices under Elizabeth, developed more and more into Puritanism from the end of the sixteenth century; and the Puritans began to agitate for a new reformation of the Church, on the principle of receding to the furthest possible distance from Catholic rites and forms. In opposition to this movement a Catholicizing school, appealing to the ancient Church, developed itself from about 1618; and through the favour of James I. and Charles I., who saw in a hierarchical organization and a strong episcopate a powerful support of the monarchy, the episcopal sees were filled with members of this school. The Laudian school, as it may be named after one of its most prominent representatives, the unfortunate Archbishop Laud, became, in the period between about 1620 and 1670, the predecessor of the "Oxford" or "Ritualistic" school of to-day, and may be said to have formed a permanent unionist academy, although matters never advanced in England to the stage of regular negotiations, as was afterwards the case in Germany. In the writings of these men, Andrewes, Montague, Laud, Bramhall, Hammond, Thorndyke, and others, we meet with manifold expressions of a desire for reunion, and a hope of its accomplishment. It would be impossible to commend the unity of the Church more eloquently and emphatically than, *e.g.* Hammond has done, who regards it as the noblest gift of God, the grace above all graces, the duty above all duties, the fulness of heavenly joy; while he regards the Churches and religious parties of his own day as the palpitating and violently dismembered limbs of a living body, which present the most revolting and painful spectacle, as though torn asunder on the rack. And the complaint constantly recurs in the works of these writers,—" If only Rome would be less hard, and not lay on us burdens we cannot bear, and make demands which are intolerable." The English bishops told Panzani, who was sent as papal agent in 1634, that two parties were labouring to hinder the union of the English and Roman Churches, viz., the Puritans and the Jesuits.[1]

But the bishops and theologians stood almost alone in the nation with their Catholic tendencies, so powerful had the Protestant spirit, in its crudest form, become in England through the influence of events, and so deeply had fear, horror, and hatred of everything connected with the Papacy sunk into the popular mind. The charge against Archbishop Laud, of having aimed at an union of the English Church with Rome, brought the primate of the Established Church to the

[1] [See above, p. 115, *note.*]

block; and it is worth remarking that his not having regarded the Pope as Antichrist formed one item in the indictment. It availed him nothing that he had declined the offer of a Cardinal's hat, and had written a learned work against the Papacy.

The Episcopal Church, closely bound up with the monarchy, shared its fall, and Puritanism triumphed with its Calvinistic doctrine, its rejection of episcopacy, sacrifice, and priesthood, and its dislike of religious symbolism and liturgical worship. But it was soon weakened by internal dissensions, three great Puritan sects—the Presbyterians, Independents, and Baptists—mutually assailing one another, and with the fall of the Commonwealth after twelve years its dominion also came to an end. At the Restoration, the Episcopal Church was re-established as well as the monarchy, and with the full approval of the nation, which was heartily sick of sectarian domination. In 1662 two thousand Puritan ministers suffered deprivation rather than submit to the ritual of the Episcopal Church, as enjoined by the Act of Uniformity, just as twelve years before many thousands of the Anglican clergy had resigned their benefices rather than accept the Puritan dogmas and forms. What a contrast with the Catholic

The English Reformation.

clergy in Elizabeth's reign, when among 9400 not 200 could be found to sacrifice their benefices rather than submit to the Protestant doctrine!

This was the sixth great change in the English Church since the beginning of the Reformation, and thenceforth its continuity has not again been interrupted, however great the fluctuation of religious views was and is among its members. The greatest change of feeling was wrought by the four years' reign of James II. He, having himself become a Catholic, did not wish, like his father and brother, to pave the way for a gradual union of the two Churches, but thought to subjugate all England to the Pope by treachery and violence, and to introduce the Jesuit type of Catholicism as the national religion—a scheme betraying a quite abnormal measure of blindness. For the English Catholics no longer formed even a hundredth part of the population, and no feeling was stronger among the overwhelming majority of the nation than hatred against the Pope and the papal Church. His policy led to the Revolution of 1688. James was dethroned, and died a fugitive in France; his descendants remained pretenders, and a German royal family, the house of Brunswick, mounted the English throne. But the result of this danger and excitement, and of lively theological controversy with Catholic divines, was to give the Church a strong impetus in the Protestant direction. At the beginning of the eighteenth century, the only representatives left of the earlier Catholicizing school were the Nonjurors, who had been thrust out of their dignities and benefices for refusing to acknowledge the new dynasty, and became extinct about the middle of the century.

Under the pressure of a still severer penal code, and the dispiriting consciousness of being objects of universal suspicion, the English Catholics constantly diminished in number, and by 1780 they had shrunk to about 65,000 in all. But towards the end of the eighteenth, and increasingly since the beginning of the present century, followed the great immigration of Irish Catholics, purchased by an oath in which at length the deposing power of the Pope was openly and expressly abjured, and in the very words of the formula of James I. It was taken by all the Bishops and Vicars-Apostolic, and Rome held her tongue. And if in our day the English Catholics number about a million, or a twentieth part of the nation, nine-tenths of them are of Irish descent. The first mitigation of the penal laws took place in 1778, but so bitter was still the popular hatred, that in 1780 there was a great outbreak in London, roused by the well-known "No-Popery" cry, (the Lord George Gordon riots), when Catholic chapels were destroyed, and the re-enactment of the penal laws was demanded of Parliament, though without success.

As a condition of complete emancipation Pitt required and obtained (in 1760) from the Theological Faculties of the Sorbonne, Louvain, Douay, Valladolid, Salamanca, and Alcala, a declaration that the Pope has no civil authority in England, that he cannot absolve from the Oath of Allegiance, and that faith must be kept with heretics.[1] And when at last, in 1824, the time of full emancipation was approaching, and the recollection of Papal Bulls, insurrections, and conspiracies of former times was found to be still the grand impediment to the bestowal of civil equality on Catholics, the English and Irish bishops issued solemn declarations to the effect that the Popes have not the slightest civil authority or any right to enforce religious duties by temporal means, such as corporal punishment and the like. This too Rome tolerated, for

[1] [The document is given at length in the Second Appendix to Sir John Cox Hippesley's *Speech on a Petition of the Irish Roman Catholics*, May 18, 1810, 2d ed., London, 1810. Cf. *Edinburgh Review*, vol. xvii. 13 *sqq.*]

emancipation depended on it. And as it involved the rejection of the theory of Papal infallibility, it was stated in the English Catechisms that this pretended Catholic doctrine was a Protestant invention.[1] But the English and Irish bishops of this day do not hold themselves bound by the words of their predecessors,

[1] [In *Keenan's Controversial Catechism*, published by "the Catholic Publishing Company, New Bond Street," and largely circulated, especially in Ireland, the following Question and Answer occur, or did occur till a twelvemonth ago, at p. 112: "*Q.* Must not Catholics believe the Pope in himself to be infallible? *A. This is a Protestant invention*; it is no article of the Catholic faith; no decision of his can oblige under pain of heresy, unless it be received and enforced by the teaching body, that is, by the Bishops of the Church." As late as August 1871 the Catechism was on sale in its original form in Dublin, but since then the leaf containing this passage has been cancelled and another substituted, in which this Question and Answer are omitted, and the book can only be obtained now in its expurgated form. As regards the testimony of the English and Irish Catholic bishops referred to in the text, the following important passage occurs in Bishop Clifford's objections to the infallibility decree, printed at Rome by authority during the Council in the *Synopsis Analytica Observationum* (see Friedrich's *Documenta Conc. Vat.*, vol. ii. p. 259) :—" Another great mischief is that before Catholics were liberated from the penal laws, and admitted to full liberty and civil equality with their fellow-citizens, bishops and theologians were publicly asked by Parliament whether the Catholics of England believed that the Pope could, without the express or implied assent of the Church, impose definitions in relation to faith or morals upon the people. All the bishops, among whom were two predecessors of his Eminence the Cardinal Archbishop of Dublin, and the theologians, answered that Catholics did not so believe. This appears in the printed papers of Parliament. In reliance on these answers the English Parliament admitted Catholics to participation in civil rights. Who will be able to persuade Protestants that Catholics have not violated honour and good faith, inasmuch as when the acquisition of civil rights was in question they publicly declared that the doctrine of Papal infallibility was no part of the Catholic faith, but as soon as they have gained what they wanted abandon their public profession of faith and assert the contrary?"]

The English Reformation.

and regard the doctrine of the episcopate of 1826 as a doctrine condemned by the present Church.

In outward form the position of the Episcopal Church in the present day is the same as in the last century. The Thirty-nine Articles and the Liturgy, which do not harmonize strictly with each other, still form the obligatory standard for its members; it still retains undisputed possession of its rich endowments, and the majority of the nation still belong to it,— an overwhelming proportion of the upper classes and rural population, but not so many of the middle class in towns. But the Dissenting communities, weakened by the disappearance of the Presbyterians,[1] but reinforced during the last hundred years by the numerous sect of Wesleyans or Methodists, are stronger and better organized in their common antagonism to the State Church than at any former period. It may still be said with truth that no Church is so national, so deeply rooted in popular affection, so bound up with the institutions and manners of the country, or so powerful in its influence on national character. During

[1] [The English Presbyterians have not disappeared altogether, though their numbers are diminished through the lapse of a large proportion into Socinianism. It was stated in the *Eclectic Review* for February 1832 that out of 258 Presbyterian congregations in England 232 had become Unitarian.—See *Letters to a Dissenter*, Seeley, p. 106.]

the last forty years it has extended its range, besides strengthening itself internally by the foundation of numerous colonial bishoprics in all quarters of the world.[1] It possesses a rich theological literature, inferior only to the German in extent and depth, and an excellent translation of the Bible, a masterpiece of style, and more accurate than the Lutheran; and it has made the Bible a people's book all over England, so that one finds it even in the bedrooms of hotels. I believe we may credit one great superiority of England over other countries to the circumstance that there the Holy Scripture is found in every house, as is the case nowhere else in the world, and is, so to speak, the good genius of the place, the protecting spirit of the domestic hearth and family. I mean that no such literature of sin and shame as has poisoned the moral atmosphere of France, and is, alas! circulated in a lesser degree in Germany, has yet found entrance into the British Isles. Another point of superiority is the observance of Sunday, which all Churches and parties have at heart, though it is not at present free from

[1] [In the *Calendar of the English Church* for 1872 I find fifty colonial dioceses enumerated, in South and West Africa, North America, Australasia, China, India, the West Indies, Sandwich Islands, and Islands of the Western Pacific.]

Judaizing exaggerations. But what I should estimate most highly is the fact that the cold, dull indifferentism, which on the Continent has spread like a deadly mildew over all degrees of society, has no place in the British Isles. To whatever extent scepticism may have advanced among the younger generation, on the whole the Englishman takes an active part in Church interests and questions, and that unnatural division and hostility between laity and clergy produced by ultramontanism in Catholic countries is quite unknown there; so much so, that the influence of the prevalent manners has extended to English Catholics, and the relations of the laity to the priesthood among them are more intimate and confidential than anywhere else. What has been accomplished during the last thirty years by the energy and generosity of religious Englishmen, set in motion and guided by the Church, in the way of popular education and church building, far exceeds what has been done in any other country.[1] Attendance at religious worship on Sunday is not, as in France, the exception but the rule with the higher and middle classes. The Church Congress at Nottingham in

[1] [The *Calendar of the English Church* for 1872 (Rivingtons) gives a list of ninety-six churches and chapels re-opened after restoration or reconstruction, and seventy-eight new ones built, during 1871 only.]

October last (1871), in which sixteen bishops and some three thousand clergymen and laymen of the most various ranks and classes took part, presented an enviable spectacle to other nations. The weightiest religious questions of the day, and the special events and difficulties of the Anglican Church, were discussed with a dignity and thoroughness which suggests to every German the tacit inquiry whether anything of the kind would be possible with us.

But there is no doubt a dark side to the picture, and three points will at once strike the eye of every observer. In the first place may be mentioned what is in England called Erastianism,—the heavy yoke of State supervision under which the English Church groans, a yoke it has indeed imposed on its own neck and daily confirms by the subscription of the Thirty-nine Articles. For this alone of all Churches in its confession of faith declares it to be a divinely revealed doctrine, that Councils cannot be held without the permission of secular princes, which implies the right of the State not to allow any authoritative declaration of doctrine without its own control and consent.[1] The King or Queen, now represented by

[1] [This is hardly accurate. The Thirty-nine Articles do not profess, like

The English Reformation.

the Privy Council, chiefly composed of laymen, is the Supreme Court of Appeal for all dogmatic or ritual questions. Its decisions in the two famous cases of Gorham and Denison[1] some years ago drove numbers of clergymen out of the Church, which seemed to them desecrated by this bondage.

A second great evil is the religious neglect of the masses congregated in the great towns. The Church, with her existing machinery, cramped by the family ties of the clergy and the want of religious corporations, feels herself powerless in the presence of this constantly increasing heathenism; and all the isolated attempts to meet the crisis have hitherto proved unavailing.

But the greatest difficulty and most painful disease of the English Church is the internal rivalry and antagonism of parties and systems, and the harassing

the Creeds, or dogmatic Canons of Councils, to deal only with revealed doctrine, but to be a formula drawn up "for the avoiding of diversities of opinion" in the public teaching of the clergy, who are alone required to subscribe them. Moreover, the 21st Article is susceptible of a different interpretation from that given in the text. See *Tract* 90 (new ed., Rivingtons, 1865), p. 21, and cf. Bishop Forbes's *Explanation of the Articles* (J. Parker, 1867), pp. 293 *sqq.*]

[1] [This is a mistake. The Denison prosecution was quashed on technical grounds at an earlier stage, and never came before the Privy Council at all on its merits. The question then raised, whether the doctrine of Transubstantiation or the "Real Objective Presence," with its consequent doctrines of sacrifice and worship, can be lawfully taught in the Church of England, was ruled affirmatively by the Judicial Committee in the recent Bennett case.]

uncertianty for clergy and laity which is its inevitable result. The divergence of views between different parties in this Church is greater than any which separates it from the Greek and Latin Churches, if the three are judged by their formal standards. Three great parties or schools are contending for mastery in the English Church,—the Evangelical or Low Church, the Broad Church, and the High Church or Anglo-Catholic. The first claims to inherit the Calvinist system, formerly naturalized in England, and to represent the principles and doctrines of the pure Protestantism of the sixteenth century. These Evangelicals are wholly destitute of theological culture, and possess and produce only a popular, not a scientific literature. The old Calvinistic doctrine of justification is to them the Alpha and Omega of Christianity. In this party is especially concentrated the old traditional hatred of the Papacy, and the anti-papal interpretation of the Apocalypse is indispensable for tickling the ears of their hearers. They still exist on the credit of their greater and more active predecessors, and by help of the institutions they founded; but they are not an advancing party, but the reverse. On the other hand, the Broad Church, as being the youngest school, are still in progress.

The English Reformation. 133

Created and sustained by the study of German philosophical and theological literature, they form an union of sympathizing scholars rather than a Church party, but exercise no inconsiderable influence on the views of educated lay society. As eclectics, they recognise in every large ecclesiastical body a mixture of truth and falsehood, good and evil, but consider the English Church the best relatively, on account of its combination of Catholic and Protestant doctrines, and the great diversity of opinion cherished within its pale. They attach little importance to the form of Church-government, but all the more to the maintenance of the union of Church and State.

The third, and from our point of view most important party, is that termed by its opponents the High Church or Ritualistic, and which calls itself the Anglo-Catholic. Its headquarters are at the University of Oxford, from which it derives its name. It repudiates the title of Protestant. It has been in process of development for forty years, and claims descent from the school of theologians of the seventeenth century, mentioned before, reaching from Andrewes to Bingham. It regards the Church as the divinely ordained organ and keeper of doctrine and the means of grace, and as standing or falling by the apostolical succession. And as this can only be found in the three great Churches whose continuity has never been interrupted,—the Western, Eastern, and English,—these three together make up the true universal Church; their substantial agreement in matters essential to salvation not being prejudiced by various excrescences, abuses, and errors which may be found in them. The body of the Church, one in origin, has in course of time, through the sin of man and by Divine permission, become divided into three great branches—outwardly separated, but inwardly united,—which, when the right time is come, will grow together again into one tree, overshadowing the world with its foliage.

The Oxford or Anglo-Catholic school does not consider itself to be at issue with the doctrinal standards of the English Church. It maintains that by God's grace the Thirty-nine Articles, apart from the opinions of their authors, were so composed as to admit of an interpretation in the sense of the ancient undivided Church, and are therefore capable of being subscribed by men holding their views. And in fact three explanations of the Articles in a Catholic sense have already appeared,—one in the seventeenth century by the Catholic theologian,

The English Reformation.

Davenport (Sancta Clara);[1] another in 1841 by John Henry Newman, who has since become a Catholic; and the last in 1867, by Forbes, Bishop of Brechin.

It is chiefly from this section of the English Church that proposals and considerations on the subject of reunion emanate. Their most influential theologian, Pusey, has undertaken to show, in his last great work, the *Eirenicon*, how comparatively easy an union would be, inasmuch as the doctrines in which both Churches agree are so many. But that was all written before the notorious decrees of the Vatican Council, the bare possibility of which nobody then believed in. The bridge for corporate union has now been broken down.

[1] [*Paraphrastica Expositio Articulorum Confessionis Anglicanæ*, edited, with Introduction and Translation, by Rev. F. G. Lee. Hayes, 1865. Christopher Davenport was born at Coventry about 1598, and matriculated at Merton College, Oxford, in 1613. He soon afterwards became a Roman Catholic, and went first to Douay, and then to Ypres, where he entered the Franciscan Order, taking the name of Franciscus a S. Clara, in 1617. In 1639, on the re-establishment of the English Franciscan province, he returned to his native country, and was appointed chaplain to the Queen, Henrietta Maria. He was the author of several theological works, and after three times holding the office of Provincial of the Order in England, died at Somerset House in 1680. The *Exposition of the Articles* was published in 1646, and dedicated to Charles I. Of the Thirty-nine Articles, Sancta Clara considers eighteen Catholic throughout, and two (11 and 12) concerned with mere logomachies, while the rest require, but also admit of, explanation in whole or in part, and these last are examined at length, viz., Articles 6, 9, 13-15, 19-22, 24, 25, 28-32, 35-37. The work is supposed to have formed the basis of the famous *Tract* 90, to which Cardinal Wiseman refers in his *Letter to Lord Shrewsbury*, as containing "*the demonstration that such interpretation may be given to the most difficult Articles as will strip them of all contradiction to the decrees of the Tridentine Synod.*"]

LECTURE VII.

DIFFICULTIES AND GROUNDS OF HOPE.

"YOU speak of a possible reunion of separated Churches, while you are yourself obliged to admit that the largest of them, which is your own, has made union with her impossible by the decrees of July 18, 1870." This is the objection before us, on which I proceed to remark as follows.

Certainly no other Church will think of uniting with a body which assumes the right, never before claimed or heard of throughout the Christian world, of making new dogmas, and places this right at the absolute disposal of a single individual. And for this reason, that in dealing with a Church so despotically constituted there cannot be any union, from the nature of the case, but only unconditional submission and renunciation of all knowledge and judgment of one's own. The notion of binding one's-self to accept articles of faith to be here-

Difficulties and Grounds of Hope. 137

after fabricated and as yet unknown, contradicts the fundamental principles of Christianity.[1]

When a great change is to be carried through, a new doctrine introduced, and a great institution revolutionized, the first question to be asked is, which side the younger generation will take? for to them belongs the future. We ask, therefore, whether our boys and youths will really become inoculated with the new doctrines, and make them, as directed, the basis of their faith, with which the whole edifice of Christianity stands or falls? Will they say, " My infallible master, my true lord and governor, to whom I am subject, body and soul, is that Italian priest who is called the Pope"? I think it impossible. It is inconceivable, because our whole education and training in Germany is an historical one, and every page of history convicts this system of spiritual absolutism of falsehood; because, in the present condition and wide spread of historical knowledge in Germany, our youth will inevitably discover that the new dogma of papal omnipotence is a

[1] [Accordingly, Archbishop Murray, of Dublin, when examined before a Parliamentary Committee in 1825 on the nature and extent of Papal prerogatives, and asked whether there had been any change in Catholic belief on the subject, replied, " *With respect to faith there can be no change ;* the faith of the Catholic Church we consider to be invariable."—*Sessional Papers*, 1825, vol. viii. p. 239]

product of fraud and forgery, and a source of ruin for Churches as well as States. It is no longer possible to shut out our youth from knowledge, to keep them in ignorance of history. In that as in many other matters they are deceived at Rome. The Italian, Spanish, South American, and French bishops, who conformed to the Pope's will on July 18, possessed indeed not the slightest particle of historical culture; but what was and is practicable in those countries, in the lamentable condition of their schools, is not possible in Germany. That circumstance alone must upset the calculations of the Vatican party, as far as Germany is concerned, for even the women and country folk, who are still reckoned upon, will be gradually and irresistibly drawn into the stream of knowledge emanating from the educated classes, and carried along with it. Our young students will either put aside the articles of faith made yesterday, in the true conviction that they will be as foreign to the future as they are to the past belief of the Church, and will adhere to the ancient doctrine, or—God grant it be not the commoner result!—on account of these untenable articles will reject the whole faith and abandon all religion.

I may be further asked how I can venture to cherish and kindle in others hopes of reconciliation, when the

Difficulties and Grounds of Hope. 139

old, well proved and implacable enemies of ecclesiastical union—the men to whom any union, which is not an unconditional surrender, is an abomination—the Jesuits, are at present more numerous and influential in Germany than in any other country. Have they not their strong fortresses and intrenched camps in the very heart of our Empire? Are they not already dominant in Westphalia and the Rhineland? Do they not keep our bishops in complete dependence on them, and have not these last just held up the Jesuits to popular encouragement and veneration, as models of Christian wisdom and virtue? Is it not they who pre-arranged the Vatican decrees, and thus, so to say, lent a hand to the Pope and the ultramontane bishops?

To this I reply as follows. I do not only believe but know that the reign of this Order in Germany will not be of long duration, that their brilliant victory —I mean especially the battles won on July 18 and August 31, 1870,[1] the Vatican decrees and surrender of the German bishops—will at no distant future be converted into a defeat. The clear testimony of history leaves no doubt about it.

[1] [The date of the second Fulda Pastoral, accepting the Vatican decrees. —Cf. Reinkens' *Unterwerfung der deutschen Bischöfe zu Fulda*, Münster, 1871. It will be remembered that this Lecture was delivered in March last.]

The experience of three centuries shows that the Jesuits have no lucky hand. No blessing ever rests on their undertakings. They build with unwearied assiduity, but a storm comes and shatters the building, or a flood breaks in and washes it away, or the worm-eaten edifice falls to pieces in their hands. The Oriental proverb about the Turks may be applied to them: "Where the Turk sets his foot, grass never grows." Their missions in Paraguay, Japan, and among the wild North American tribes have long since gone to ruin. In Abyssinia they had once (in 1625) almost attained dominion, but soon afterwards (in 1634) the whole concern collapsed, and they never ventured to return there. What is left to-day of their laborious missions in the Levant, the Greek islands, Persia, the Crimea, and Egypt? Scarcely a reminiscence of their former presence there is to be found on the spot.

Above all has the Society of Jesus devoted its best services to its native home of Spain. Themselves children of the Spanish race and inheritors of the Spanish character, for sixty years they displayed their Spanish feeling throughout Europe; they laboured for the spread and consolidation of the universal monarchy of Spain. The result was the bankruptcy and depopulation of that once powerful kingdom, and its loss of one possession after another, so that by the end of the seventeenth century, to cite the language of a Spanish writer, it had become an inanimate corpse, the skeleton of a giant. In Spain itself they co-operated with the Inquisition for two hundred years in impressing their spirit on the life of the people, with this result, that the higher education has been crushed, the scientific spirit strangled, and the country, ruined in every department of life, is still behind every other country in Europe except Turkey, and, having no healthy literature of its own, has to feed on the foreign literature of France. Well might a Spanish diplomatist in Rome say, at the time of the suppression of the Order, "The Jesuits are the wood-worm that gnaws on our bowels."[1]

They it was who brought on the German nation the Thirty Years' War and its results, and to them Catholic Germany owes the decline of its schools and its consequent backwardness in cultivation and long intellectual sterility. It was they who completely undermined the ancient German and Catholic Empire, and paved the way for its fall. They, as the all-powerful conscience-

[1] "Quanto bien nos ha di venir de la expulsion de la carcoma que nos roea las entranas."—*Espiritù di Azara*, p. 26.

keepers of the Hapsburgs, Ferdinand I., Ferdinand II., and Leopold I., have on their conscience the destruction of the liberties of the States of the Empire, the thorough enforcement of absolutism, the oppression and expulsion of the Protestants; in a word, that whole crop of inextinguishable hatred which the house of Hapsburg has sown throughout Protestant Germany. By their influence that intellectual quarantine was established, by which the Austrian states have been entirely cut off from the rest of Germany, German culture kept at arm's length, and that exclusion of Austria brought about which we have lived to witness.

Bohemia has long been given over to the care and charge of the Jesuits, and what have they made of it? They have utterly destroyed the old Czech literature, and have brought matters to such a pass that nearly the whole Bohemian nobility is annihilated through executions, confiscations, and banishment, three thousand families driven out of the country, and the Bohemian constitution broken up. And now the harvest of the dragon's teeth sown by the Order of Loyola is springing up, and if the contest of the two nationalities there admits of no peace or reconciliation, the acts of the seventeenth century and their authors must bear the blame. The working of the Order in the ecclesiastical principalities may be exemplified from the condition of the electoral state of Cologne, as recently described by Perthes. There for nearly two centuries everything was subject to their influence and direction, as confessors of the Electors.

In England the destiny of the Catholics was for a century moulded by the influence of the Jesuits at Rome and the intense hatred which they excited at home, and we have seen what a monstrous weight of misfortune and oppression they rolled down on the shoulders of their hapless co-religionists.

They tried to reintroduce Catholicism into Sweden by means of a liturgy forcibly imposed on the clergy, and with the help of King Sigismund, who was under their guidance; Sigismund in consequence lost his crown, and they were banished for ever from the country.[1]

In Russia they undertook, by means of their instrument, the false Demetrius, to establish Polish influence, and bring the Empire and nation into subjection to the See of Rome, but their proselyte and *protégé* was killed, and they had to quit the country. In Poland

[1] Gejer's *Geschichte Schwedens*.

they dominated the kings, the higher clergy, and the nobility for a long time; and Poland is destroyed.

In Portugal they had King Sebastian entirely in their hands, and he lost his army and his life in Africa, in a foolish campaign suggested by religious enthusiasm, and plunged his country into an abyss of misery and ruin, from which it has never been able to rise to its former prosperity. Then they did their best to promote the Spanish dominion over Portugal, and that also soon collapsed. And when they again became powerful through having the Sovereigns under their spiritual direction, the country sank into a decline, from which it is still suffering, through their intolerable misgovernment.

In France the Jesuits were the conscience-keepers of the Bourbons, and their spiritual children, Louis XIV. and Louis XV., paved the way for the Revolution and the destruction of the dynasty, or rather, one may say, made it inevitable. For the deep decay of the country, the neglect of the greater part of the nation, and the profligacy spreading from the Court, impressed on the first acts of the Revolution the destructive character which has to this day hindered the recovery of France. And here too we must say of the French Church, that

Difficulties and Grounds of Hope. 145

it was the Jesuits who, during the time they ruled it by means of the royal patronage, so devastated and demoralized it, that even in the eighteenth century it was powerless to cope with Voltairianism, and was already falling to pieces before it was finally overthrown by the Revolution.

I readily leave to this Order the fate of the Vatican decrees, the more readily as it has the duties of paternity to discharge towards them. For the Jesuits excogitated, sketched out, and finally shaped those decrees, though with the assistance of certain Bishops.

And now I turn to the friends of our cause, those who have before me borne their testimony to it, and those on whose co-operation or sympathy we may reckon.

There are three works of recent date occupied with the question of the union of the Churches, all of which have fed my hopes and raised my courage ; for they prove that alike in Germany and in England the number of the friends of union is by no means small, and is still increasing. The author of *Pax Vobiscum*[1] is an influential clergyman in Franconia. He paints in glaring colours the great and almost insuperable

[1] *Pax Vobiscum. Die kirchliche Wiedervereinigung der Katholiken und Protestanten historish-pragmatisch beleuchtet von einem Protestanten.* Bamberg, 1863.

difficulties which beset every step on the road to reunion. There does not seem to him either the capacity or the call to accomplish the blessed work at the present time, but the way should be prepared for it, and every impediment, as far as possible, got rid of.[1] Nor does he conceal that the contest for dear life which both Churches will have to carry on, against the giant powers of unbelief and destruction which are rising up against them, can only be waged successfully with their forces united.

The second work, by the Berlin preacher Schulze, goes so far in the approval and acceptance of Catholic doctrines that one may almost say that, if it expressed the mind of a preponderating majority in the German Protestant Church, four-fifths of the difficult work of reunion would be already accomplished.[2] Nor does the work stand alone, as is shown by the fact that the *Evangelische Kirchenzeitung* of Berlin for 1870 has communicated and indorsed its contents.

The third work, by Dr. Pusey, the views of which are substantially shared by thousands of the clergy and laity of the Anglican Church, goes further still than

[1] *Pax Vobiscum*, p. 342.
[2] *Ueber romanisirende Tendenzen, ein Wort zum Frieden.* Berlin, 1870.

Schulze's, for the famous Oxford theologian thinks that all the doctrinal decisions of Trent might be accepted, if only certain decrees were authoritatively explained in the sense of the more moderate Catholic divines.[1] Only the extension of the papal primacy to an unlimited supremacy, and the excesses in Marian worship, and in the veneration of Saints and sacred pictures, are, in the author's eyes, the great stumbling-blocks that must first be removed.

We constantly hear complaints now of a general hostility to the Church. There is said to be a widespread feeling of alienation and dislike towards her, variously and injuriously manifested in the press and in society. That such complaints should be made on the Catholic side is perfectly intelligible. The party now dominant in the Church is warlike and aggressive, and constantly proclaims that it is striving for two great objects.[2] In the first place, it is resolved to rule and subjugate everything, not only in the sphere of

---

[1] *An Eirenicon.* By Rev. E. B. Pusey, D.D. Rivingtons, 1865. Cf. *First Letter to Very Rev. J. H. Newman, D.D.*, 1869, and *Is Healthful Reunion impossible? a Second Letter*, etc., 1870.

[2] [Compare Newman's description of the action of this same "insolent and aggressive faction," in his letter to Bishop Ullathorne, published in the *Standard* of April 7, 1870. It is quoted in full at pp. 355 *sqq.* of *Letters of Quirinus.* Rivingtons, 1870.]

religious but of moral and even political and civil life. In the next place, it is resolved to undermine, and, when the right moment arrives, to destroy the existing public order of society and modern legislation, with the liberty of the press, of religion, of teaching, etc.; for with these things—appealing as it does to the principles of the Syllabus and the views of the Popes—it cannot reconcile itself. But with the Protestant Church it is different. Its clergy, allowing of course for some exceptions, can neither be charged with lust of power nor with hostility to the present order of society. And here I am reminded of the strong saying uttered at a Church meeting: "We have no flocks at our back; ninety-nine hundredths of our people are in league with the enemy."[1] How is this phenomenon to be explained? And how is one to explain another cognate phenomenon, which I will describe in the words used by a distinguished Protestant divine, Brückner, in an address delivered at Leipsic in 1860: "Our Church, notwithstanding all remaining differences, is in many respects reverting to the condition of the age before Constantine. Public opinion is again, on the whole, enlisted, not on the side of Christianity, but

[1] Messner's *Neue Evang. Kirchenzeitung*, 1866, p. 6.

Difficulties and Grounds of Hope. 149

against it," etc.; and he anticipates oppression and sufferings for his Church.[1]

Here it is obvious that mere naked unbelief or hostility to positive religion will not explain the phenomenon; the mischief lies deeper. The general superintendent and Court preacher at Berlin, Hoffmann, has lately written on the "Causes of the antagonism to the Church in Germany."[2] He enumerates many, but above all the uncertainty and discordance of the doctrines delivered from the pulpit. The impression left on one's mind is, that the evil lies in the want of confidence and respect of the laity for their preacher, in whom they see a man teaching simply according to the measure of his attainments, and from his own subjective point of view. They have no feeling that he is supported on the broad stream of Christian tradition flowing down through eighteen centuries, and that his message is but the echo of the voice of the whole Church reaching up to Christ; that they do but hear from his mouth what has been always and everywhere proclaimed in the name of the Lord. If then the German Protestant

[1] *Die Kirche nach ihr. Ursprung, Geschichte, Gegenwart, Vorträge,* von Luthardt, Kahnis und Brückner. Leipsic, 1865.

[2] See his periodical, *Deutschland,* Jahrg. i. pp. 224 *sqq.*

Church was enlarged by union with other Churches, and re-entered by this union with the ancient Churches into their unbroken continuity of Church life and doctrine, would she not gain in strength and authority? Would not her testimony be weightier and her power of popular attraction increased?

If we look closer, we shall be able to assume a disposition and readiness for union among all those who admit that the communion they belong to is not absolutely the Church, the one and single Church complete in itself, but only a branch Church, which cannot claim to be itself that One Holy Catholic and Apostolic Church whereof the Creed speaks. This is maintained by those divines who adhere most strictly to the Lutheran doctrine.[1] They, as well as most Protestant theologians at the present day, say that there is no communion of which it can be affirmed that the fulness of the gifts of grace and spiritual life dwell exclusively within its pale, while all without is apostasy and heresy.[2] It follows that they must hold the one Catholic Church to be now split into fragments, each of the great Churches having, of course in different degrees, its

[1] So Harnack, *Die Kirche, ihr Amt, ihr Regiment*, Nürnberg, 1862, pp. 87 *sqq.*

[2] Cf. Stahl, *Die lutherische Kirche und die Union*, p. 450.

Difficulties and Grounds of Hope.   151

peculiar advantages and defects. But it also follows that no single Church can claim Catholicity to the exclusion of the rest. The Greek and Russian Churches do not do so. Mouravieff observes that the Councils held in the East by Greek and Russian Bishops had abstained from calling themselves " Œcumenical," because the Greek Church cannot regard herself as the universal Church apart from the Roman.[1]

And here I will refer to a doctrinal ruling of Catholic theology, which is admitted even by the most papally-minded theologians, and which as I believe may be of the greatest service for the cause of union. It is always taught in the Church that baptism is what makes every one a member of the true Catholic Church, and as baptism can never be obliterated or repeated, anybody once baptized remains for ever a member of the One Church, even should he pass over to another sect or Church, only that he then loses the rights of membership. In the religious manual approved by Church authority for use in the Bavarian schools, it is

[1] *Question Religieuse d'Orient et d'Occident* (Moscow, 1856), pp. 223. [Similarly the Popes who summoned the Councils of Lyons and Florence for the reunion of the Greeks, Gregory X. and Eugenius IV., speak throughout in their official documents of "the union of the Western and Eastern Church," of "uniting the Church of God," etc. See, for the detailed evidence of this, Ffoulkes's *Christendom's Divisions*, pp. 259-261, 337-340.]

taught that those who have been made members of Christ by the sacrament of baptism, if they remain out of her visible communion only through involuntary ignorance and error, are regarded by the Church as her true children erring by no fault of their own.

And here it must be explained that the notion of involuntary error is a very wide one, for it includes all who cannot be charged with obstinacy (*pertinacia*) and conscious rejection of recognised truth. Consequently the great majority of Protestants are members of the One Catholic Church. Of the eighty million Greeks and Russians this is self-evident. So broad is the notion of Catholicity, and thus disappears what else would be offensive and odious in the maxim, " Out of the Church no salvation." Certainly Pius VIII. in his Brief of March 25, 1830, addressed to the Rhenish Bishops, has again enjoined on them the teaching of this doctrine in the harshest sense, and without the addition of any mitigating or explanatory interpretation, and that with direct reference to the Protestants.[1] But Pius IX. has not thought himself bound by this judgment, and declares in an Allocution of December 9, 1854, not only, first, that ignorance is an excuse before

[1] Denziger, *Eincheiridion Symb. et Defin.*, 1854, p. 423.

Difficulties and Grounds of Hope. 153

God, but, secondly, that "no one can undertake to fix the limits of this ignorance, when regard is had to the diversity of peoples, countries, and minds, and the influence of many other circumstances." The Pope therefore teaches, or must by logical inference teach and inculcate, " Judge not that ye be not judged ; condemn no one who is in error according to your opinion, for you cannot tell whether his error is inculpable or not." That the prevalent practice in the Roman Catholic Church and the conduct of many of her priests is in glaring contradiction to these theories, is perfectly true. If Popes and Bishops wished to be consistent, they would be obliged to acknowledge that the Church is obscured and her visible evidence and attractive power lessened by the gross abuses prevalent, the amount of superstitions favoured and practised, and the spectacle of so many scandals among the clergy, and that this excuses before God the judgment of those who refuse the invitation to enter her communion. But this doctrine of the Church being partly visible and partly invisible does us excellent service, first, in disposing of the old controversy between Catholic and Protestant theologians about the visibility or invisibility of the Church ; and secondly, because it enables us to say to all members of other communions,

"As being baptized, we are all on either side brothers and sisters in Christ, we are all at bottom members of the universal Church. In this great garden of God let us shake hands with one another over the confessional hedges, and let us break them down so as to be able to embrace one another altogether. These hedges are the doctrinal divisions, about which either we or you are in error; if you are wrong, we do not hold you morally culpable, for your education, surroundings, knowledge, and training make your adhering to these doctrines excusable, and even right. Let us examine, compare, and investigate the matter together, and we shall discover the precious pearl of religious peace and Church unity, and then join our hands and forces in cleansing and cultivating the garden of the Lord, which is overgrown with weeds."

The doctrine of conversion and justification is still regarded in many quarters as the most important point of difference. It was, men say, the turning-point of the German Reformation, its fairest jewel and speciality, the article of a standing or falling Church. The words of the Elector of Brandenberg are often cited, who impressed above all on the consciences of his theologians, when setting off for a conference with their

Difficulties and Grounds of Hope. 155

opponents, to bring back with them the little word "sola," *i.e.* the doctrine that man is justified by faith "alone." And in fact this doctrine formed the principal subject of the public discussions at diets and religious conferences, as at Ratisbon in 1541 and 1546. But I must confess, at the risk of manifold contradictions, that this is just the point where reconciliation seems to me most easily attainable. On one side are ranged the whole Western Catholic Church, the whole Greek and Russian Church, and the greater part of the Anglican Church; all these adhere to the ancient doctrine. The Protestant doctrine, as it is most clearly taught in the two Formularies of Concord and the Catechism of Heidelberg, is no doubt absolutely irreconcilable with the doctrine of the other Churches. The contradiction is so glaring and decisive, that, were the Protestant doctrine adhered to, all hope of reunion must be given up. But happily this is not the case; the overwhelming majority of German Protestant divines, and especially those who make Scripture exegesis their speciality, only differ in their manner of expression, and not in substance, from the ancient doctrine.[1]

[1] [See, for some illustrations of this, my *Catholic Doctrine of the Atonement*, pp. 281-284.]

The celibacy of the clergy can form no ground of separation, for this reason, if for no other, that even the Roman Church does not regard it as a divine law, but only as an ecclesiastical ordinance, and does not therefore hesitate to hold communion with the married clergy of the Eastern Church. And, on the other hand, Protestants, remembering certain exhortations of St. Paul, ought to allow that it well befits the Church to have a class of ministers who voluntarily renounce family life, in order to devote themselves exclusively to the service of the flock, and to offer to that body of the laity who, in these days, are compelled by poverty or their station in life to remain unmarried, an example of continence which might else be represented as impossible.

So again with communion in both kinds. The withdrawal of the chalice in Western Christendom has caused unspeakable mischief, and led to divisions and wars; nor have I been able to discover any important benefit resulting from it. The whole Eastern and Russian Church, Uniate as well as Orthodox, administers communion under both species; and at all events those Churches which are willing to unite ought not to be rejected on that account.

Difficulties and Grounds of Hope. 157

As regards the doctrine of the intermediate state, it is clear how both Churches might gain by comparing and coming to an understanding on their points of difference. Protestant theologians complain that the popular notion of two states only after death—heaven and hell, immediate beatitude or damnation,—and the consequent disuse of prayer for the departed, "has brought the people to the brink of doubt about eternal life altogether."[1] They acknowledge that belief in an intermediate state of cleansing ought to be received, and prayer for the dead recommended, even for the sake of the living, and indeed ought to be formally reintroduced.[2] On the other hand, the Latin Church, by uniting with the Eastern, has allowed the scholastic opinion of a material fire in Purgatory as the means of chastisement to drop;[3] and the substance of the doctrine can cause no further offence, if once the gross abuses and misapprehensions are removed, which have incrusted its kernel in practice and popular belief.

[1] Neumann in the *Zeitschrift für luther. Theologie*, 1852, p. 282.

[2] So Karsten and F. W. Schulze. [The testimony of two other eminent Lutheran divines, Martensen and Rothe, are cited to the same effect in my *Catholic Doctrine of the Atonement* (2d ed., W. H. Allen), pp. 282, 284, and the list might easily be enlarged. For a catena of Anglican authorities in favour of prayer for the dead—which might be indefinitely lengthened by reference to living writers—see ch. xi. of *Christian Doctrine of Prayer for the Departed*, by Rev. F. G. Lee. Strahan, 1872.]

[3] [Cf. *supra*, p. 51.]

As regards confession, it is enough to remember that the need for some institution securing to the clergyman the opportunity of acting directly on the conscience of the individual Christian is keenly felt in every Church. In the Anglican Church, confession, in the strict sense of the word, has been largely practised for some years. In the German Protestant Church, as far as I can gather from its literature, there is a very widely spread desire to replace the general confession, which has become unmeaning and mechanical, by something much more like the Catholic form.

Then again, the Sacrifice of the Eucharist, and the necessity or fitness of making it the centre of public worship, as in the ancient Churches, has in our day found zealous advocates among German Protestant theologians. On the other hand, the Catholic theologians will not deny that the use of the living and universally understood language of the people is preferable to the dead Latin, which only fosters the popular fancy of some occult sacredness and magical power residing in unintelligible forms.[1]

Among the points in which the Churches have come

[1] [In the North of Germany it is very common at High Mass to sing vernacular paraphrases of the *Kyrie, Gloria, Credo*, etc., in which the people join, instead of the Latin; and authorized forms are published for this purpose in many dioceses.]

nearer than before must be reckoned the monastic institute. It is allowed by Protestants that "only by such corporations can the wants be satisfied, which always make themselves imperatively felt in the Christian community;"[1] and in fact the Protestant deaconesses correspond to the Sisters of Mercy in the Catholic Church.[2] And we may recognise an unmistakeable approximation and removal of old causes of offence in the circumstance that in the Catholic Church the female orders and convents, designed exclusively for a life of prayer and contemplation without active work, have disappeared, or are in course of disappearing; while the communities devoted to the bodily and spiritual good of others, the care of the sick and education, display a power and activity hitherto unknown.

We must make up our minds to encountering numberless adversaries. Three classes especially will set themselves to oppose our eirenic efforts,—the first numerous and powerful in England and America, the second in Germany, the third everywhere. First come all those who recognise in the Pope the fulfil-

[1] Rothe's *Ethik*, vol. iii. p. 424.

[2] [The *Calendar of the English Church* for 1872 gives between forty and fifty Anglican sisterhoods or convents, discharging various works of mercy, corporal and spiritual; some of them having several daughter houses in different localities.]

ment of the scriptural prophecies about the great enemy of Christ and the Apostasy, and consequently think no further reformation of the papal Church possible, but look for its judgment and destruction. Secondly, there are those theologians to whom the ancient doctrines common to all Christian Churches are already a burden and offence, of which they are anxious to rid themselves. The third hostile army, and its name is legion, consists of those encamped under the papal and Jesuit banner. That no stone will be left unturned by that party to hinder every approximation, and strangle at its birth every idea of peace, is certain. The Vatican Council was organized for the express purpose of making all plans of reunion for ever impossible. Individual conversions, indeed, are gladly welcomed; they are drops at once absorbed and lost in the ocean of Roman uniformity. But there is to be no negotiation on a larger scale, for bodies of men meeting on equal terms. Some years ago a society was formed in England of Anglicans and Catholics combined for the common furtherance of the union of the Christian Churches, and it was condemned by the Pope, at the instance of Archbishop Manning.[1]

[1] [The "Association for the Promotion of the Unity of Christendom" by

At the beginning, then, of any eirenic movement, its opponents will outnumber its friends and helpers. But we may count on the sympathy, if not the active help, of those who have at heart the greatness and unity of Germany, and who believe that the political union is but half the work and requires an ecclesiastical union of all its tribes as the completion, fulfilment, and crowning of the edifice. In Germany the two religions are constantly becoming more intermingled, and the artificial devices for keeping them apart are more and more felt to be disturbing and hindering influences, superseded by the movement and needs of the present, and are being gradually put aside. It seemed, after the controversy on the subject at Cologne in 1839 and the following years, as if marriages between Catholics and Protestants would become more infrequent, but they have increased of late years, and will certainly continue to increase. And these multiplying marriages and families of mixed

intercessory prayer, founded Sept. 8, 1857, and condemned by a decree of the Roman Inquisition, Sept. 16, 1864, first published in England by Archbishop Manning, shortly after his appointment to the See of Westminster, in a Pastoral dated Epiphany 1866. The official report, published by the Secretary of the Association in Sept. 1868, gives the total number of members as 12,684, including "Roman Catholics, 1881; Orientals, 685; members of miscellaneous Protestant communities, 92; of Church of England, 10,026."—See *Union Review*, vol. vii. p. 74.]

religion are already paving the way for the fusion of the Churches, and encourage us not to lose heart. The mixture and interpenetration of the adherents of the two confessions advances unchecked. There are no longer any towns, and there will in time be no villages, where Catholics and Protestants are not dwelling side by side. But that mutual tolerance and respect which depends on the forms of refined social intercourse is confined to the higher and educated classes. Among the lower classes and the country population the intermixture of confessions must either lead to a coarse unbelieving indifferentism, or beget the desire and need for a Church union, which may put an end to those interminable religious troubles, frictions, and asperities.

I have found it the almost universal conviction in foreign countries that it is the special mission of Germany to take the lead in this world-wide question, and give to the movement its form, measure, and direction. We are the heart of Europe, richer in theologians than all other lands; and the linguistic knowledge indispensable for this task exists with us in a higher degree than anywhere else. What can, what ought to be done? A negotiation between the

Difficulties and Grounds of Hope. 163

Churches through plenipotentiaries accredited on either side promises no result; the mere proposal or attempt would now, after July 18, 1870, be a folly. The right instruments would be found in men, both of the clergy and laity, who would unite for common action, first in Germany, untrammelled by instructions, and simply following their own mind and judgment. They would soon draw others to them in rapidly increasing numbers, by the magnetic power of a work so pure and pleasing to God, and would thus be brought into communication with like-minded men in other countries. The basis of their consultations would be Holy Scripture, with the three œcumenical Creeds, interpreted by the still undivided Church of the early centuries. Thus would an international society of the noblest and most beneficial kind be formed, and what began as a snowball might well become an irresistible avalanche. There would be no lack of cold contempt or furious hostility to the work; but they would fail to overthrow it.

A Prussian official, who had long been concerned with the ecclesiastical affairs of both Confessions, wrote thus at the end of his public career in 1857:—"I am certain the time will come, before the newly inserted stones are mouldered, when a common Te Deum will be sung in the cathedral of Cologne."[1]

In this belief and hope I desire to live and die. Nor could I wish for any better success and reward of my Lectures than this; that my hearers should make a like hope part of their life, carry it into their dealings with members of other communions, and, wherever an opportunity occurs of bearing witness to it, not remain cold and dumb. We Germans have lived to see days of serious import and joyful triumph,—days of victory and of national unity at length attained; and I trust that our people will remain strong enough and moral enough to maintain the lofty position divine Providence has assigned to them. But these days of triumph have had to be dearly bought with terrible sacrifices, and at the cost of rivers of human blood. Here, in the sphere of religion and in the effort for religious peace, a fairer crown and bloodless victory awaits the German people,—more difficult indeed to win than that victory over France, for it is the conquest of ourselves, our indolence, our pride, our selfishness, our prejudices, our easy self-conceit. But if we are willing to march to this contest, we march under a

[1] Eilers, *Meine Wanderung durch Leben* (Leipsic, 1857), vol. ii. p. 265.

Leader whose name may inspire the most faint-hearted with courage. It is He from whom descends every good and perfect gift, whose word is not yet fulfilled, but must be fulfilled in time to come : " There shall be one fold and one Shepherd."

PRINTED BY T. AND A. CONSTABLE, PRINTERS TO HER MAJESTY,
AT THE EDINBURGH UNIVERSITY PRESS.